I0480599

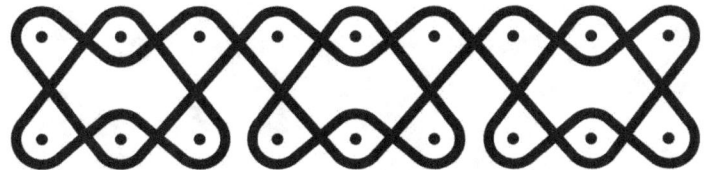

Dot To Dot Mindfulness

A unique activity book for

hand mind coordination in children and adults

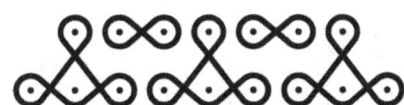

Ramya Srinivasan

Copyright©**2021** Ramya Srinivasan
All Rights Reserved
All inquiries about this book can be sent to the author at
ramyaprasannabooks@gmail.com

See this

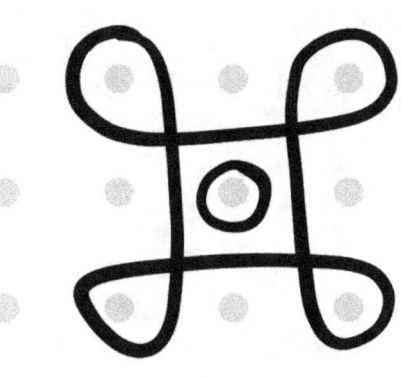

And draw here..

Practice pages

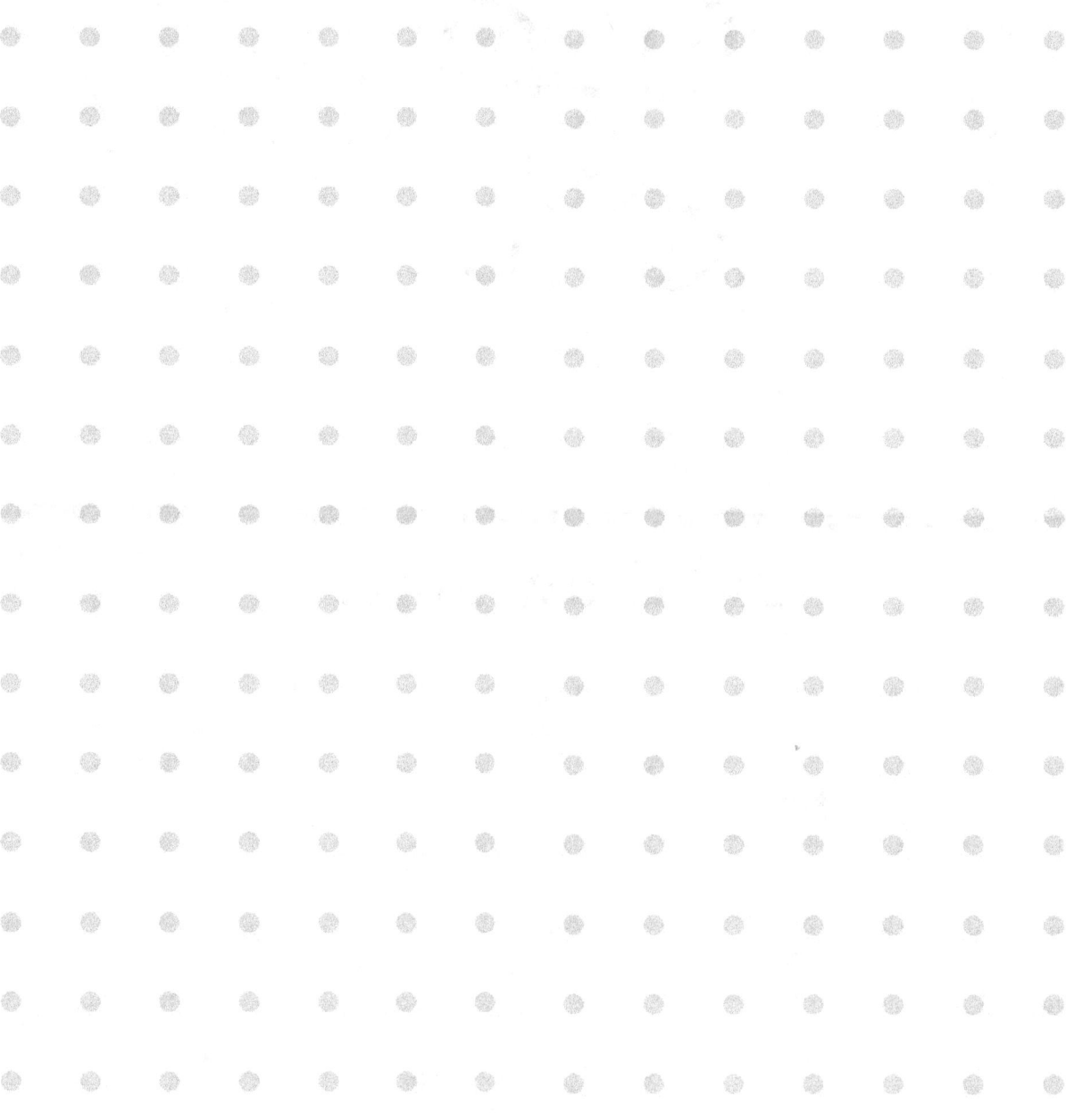

See this

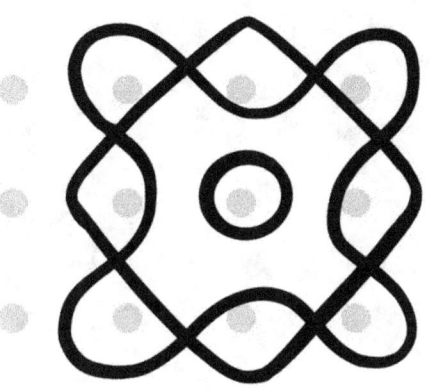

And draw here..

Practice pages

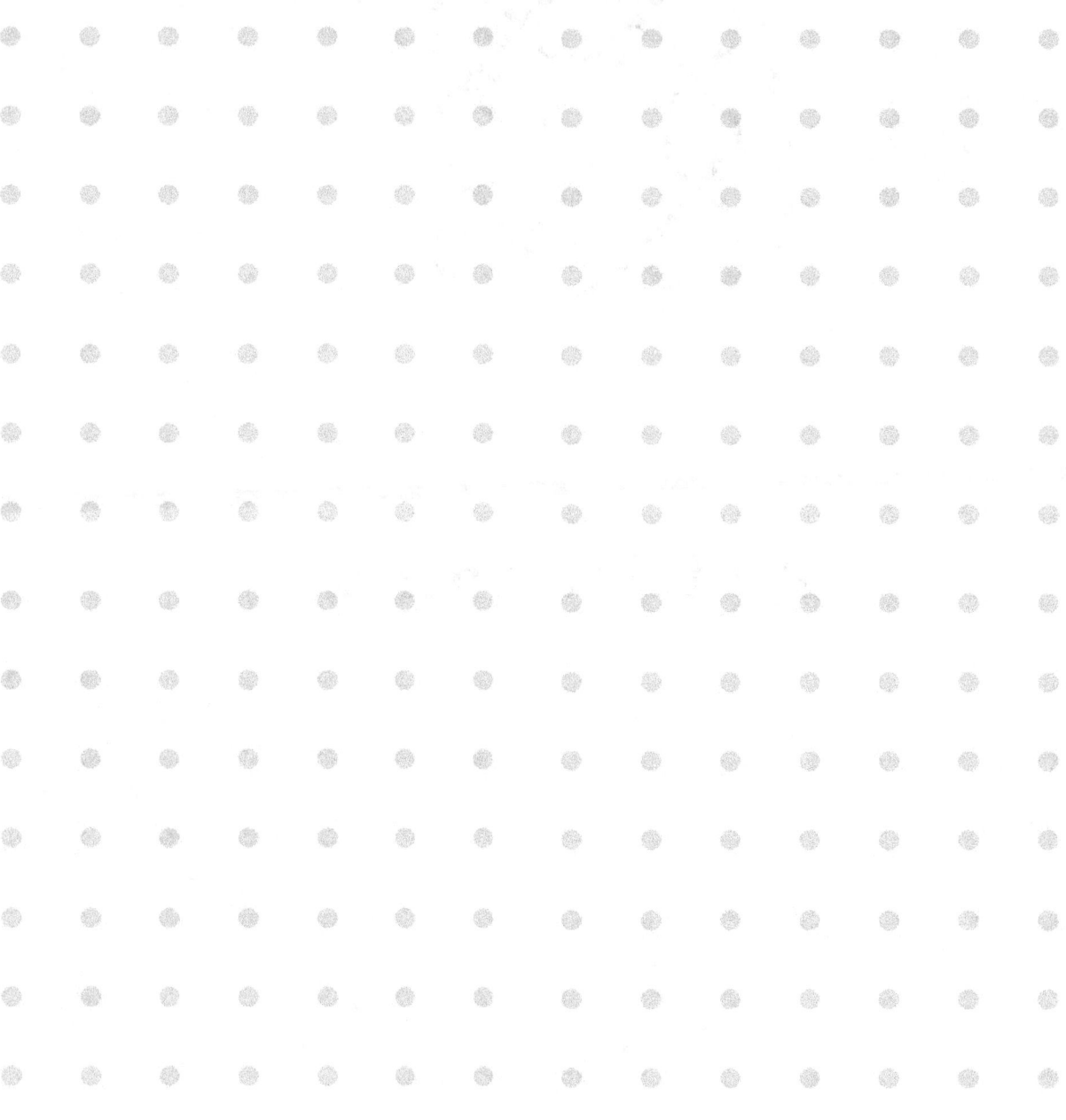

See this

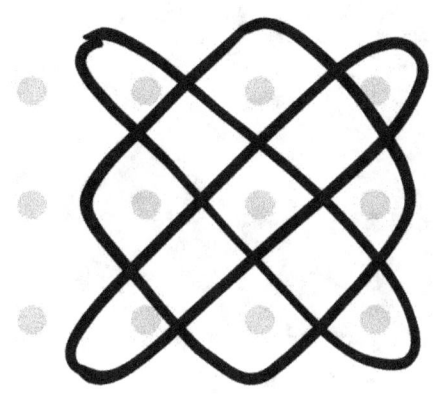

And draw here..

Practice pages

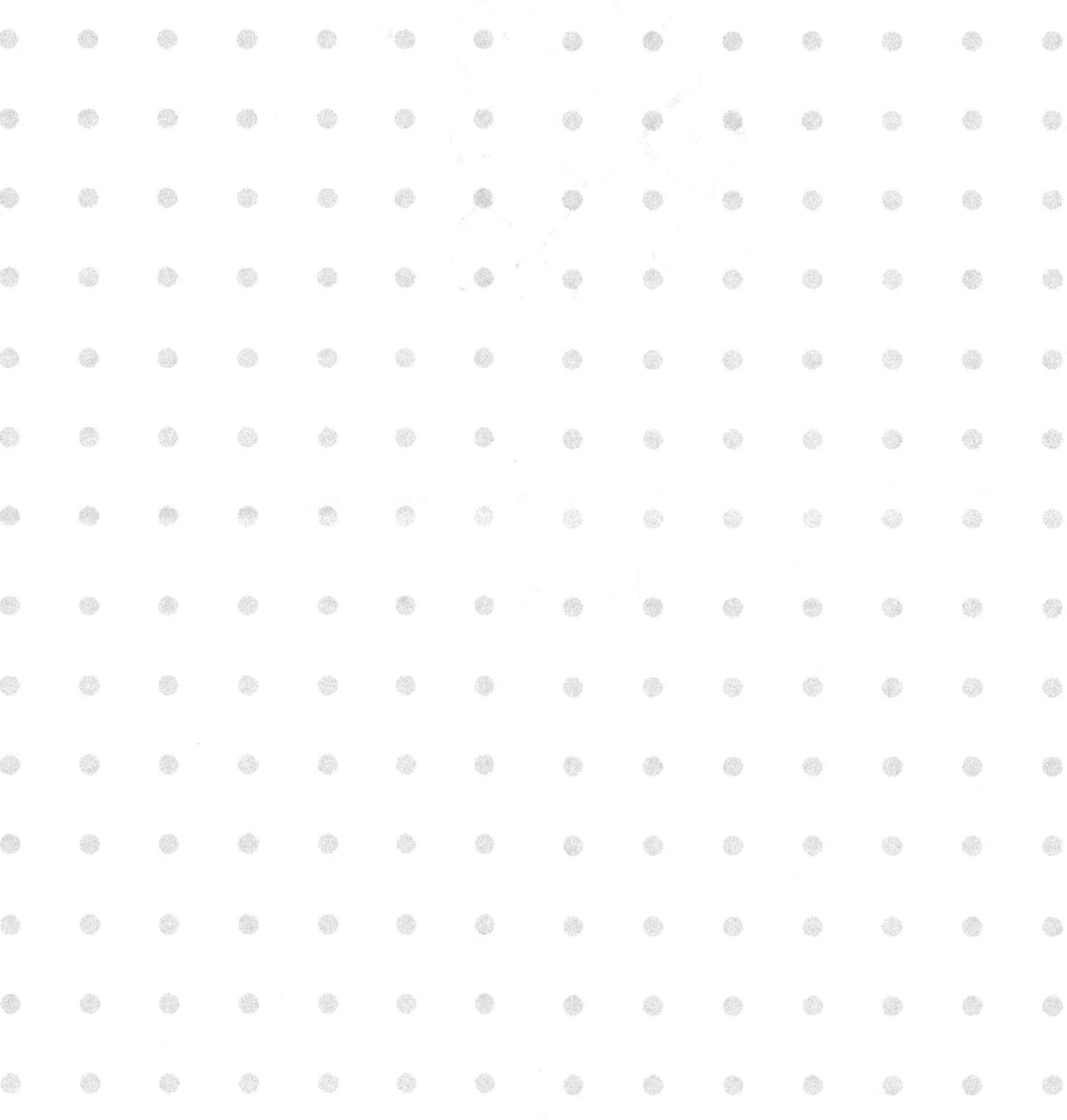

See this

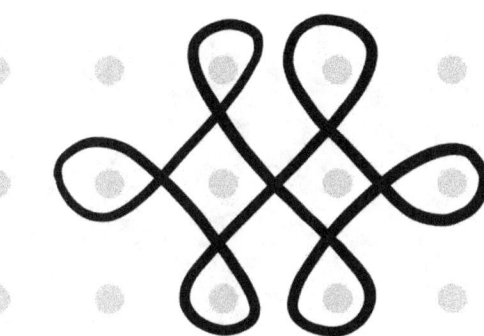

And draw here..

Practice pages

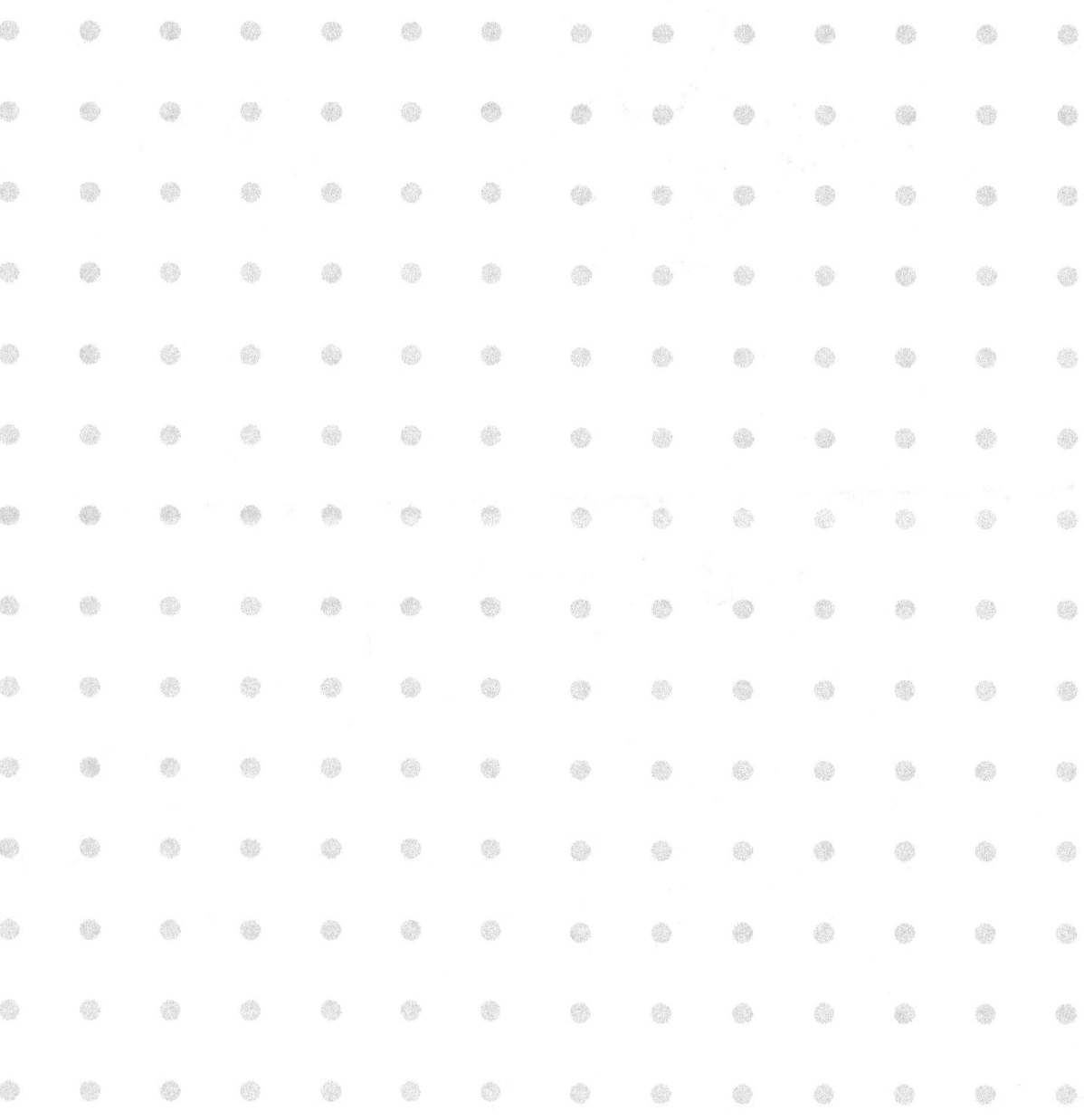

See this

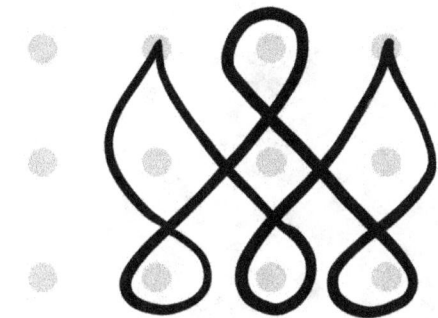

And draw here..

Practice pages

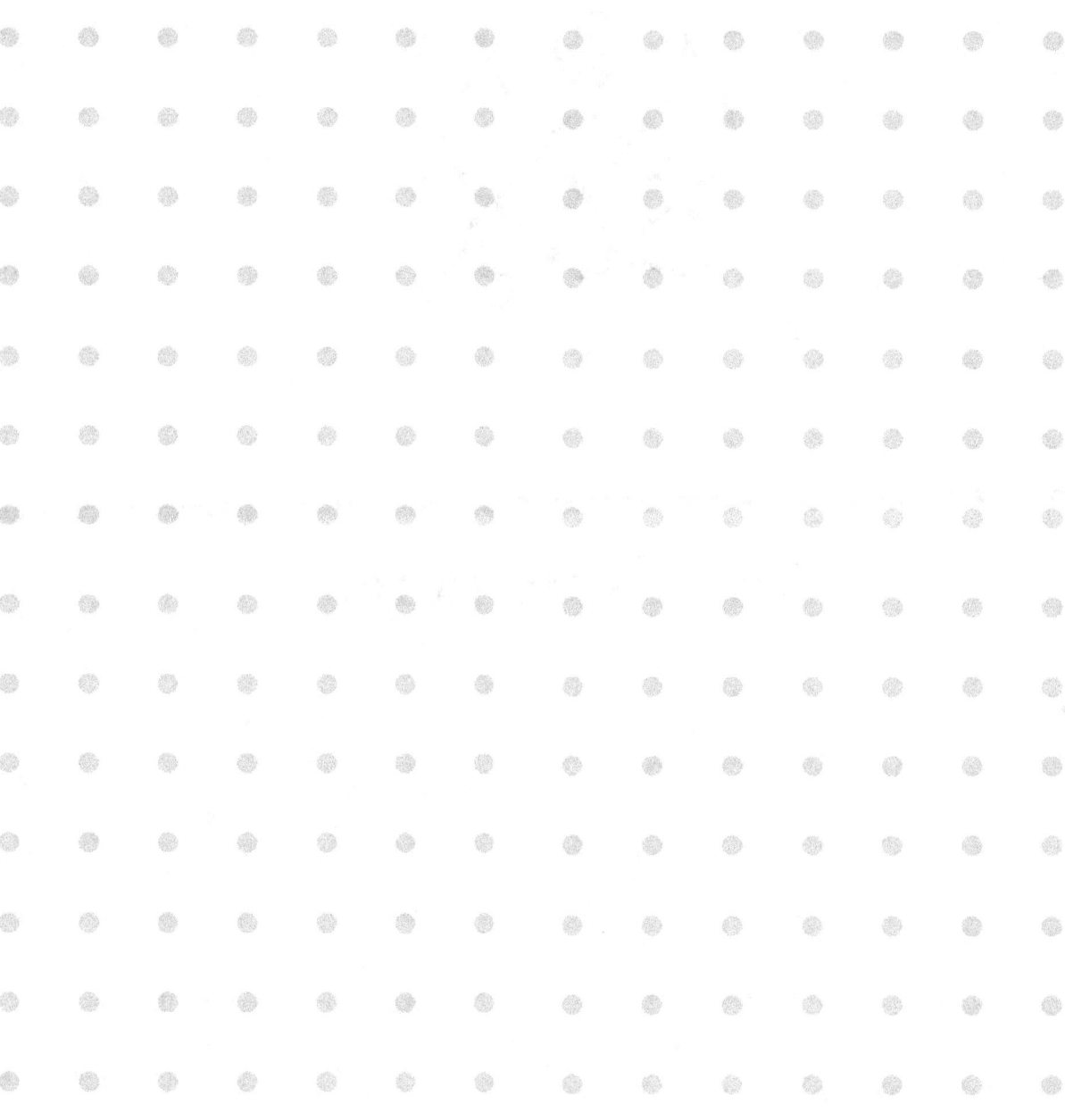

See this

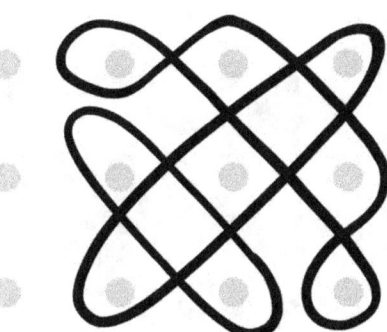

And draw here..

Practice pages

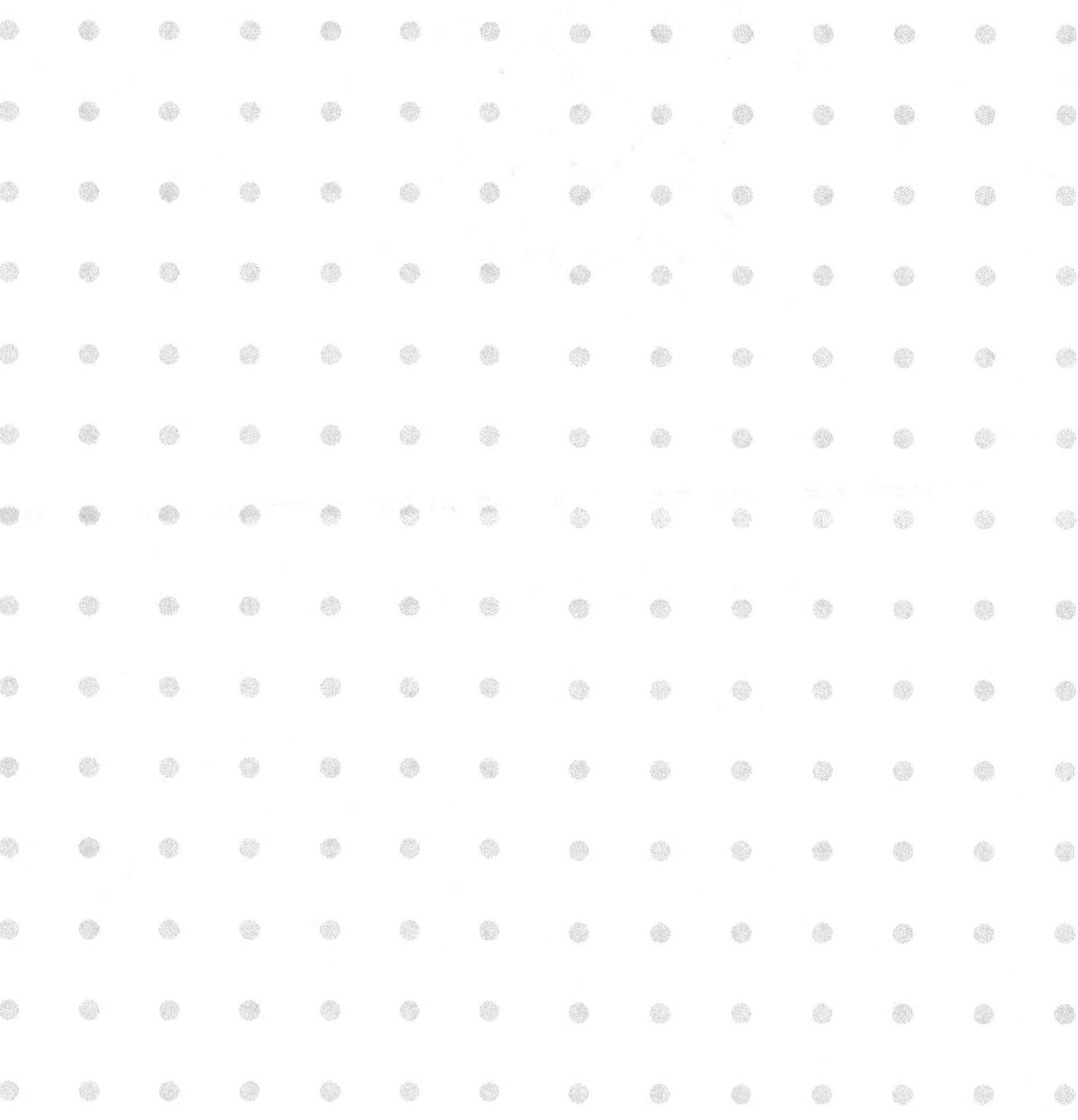

See this

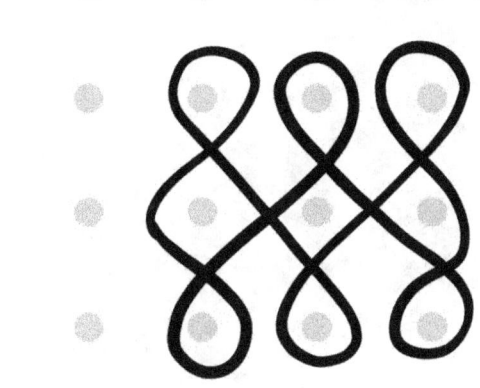

And draw here..

Practice pages

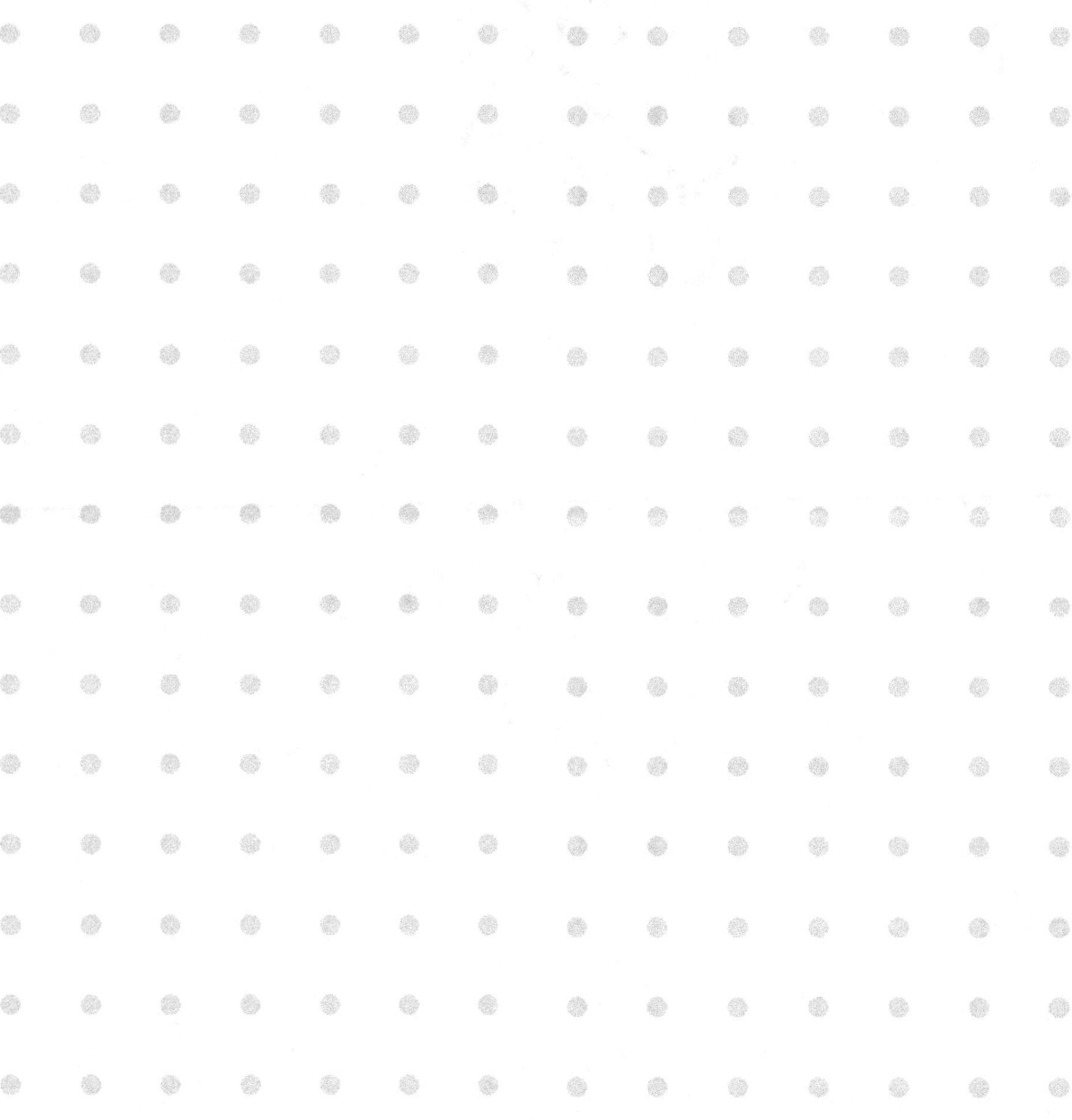

See this

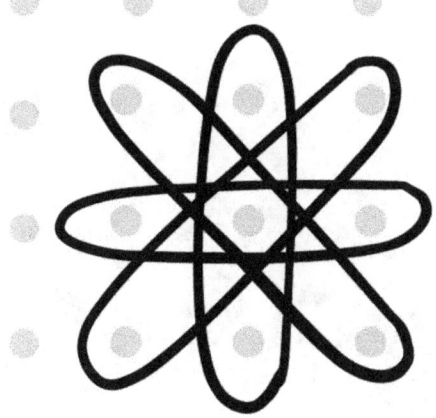

And draw here..

Practice pages

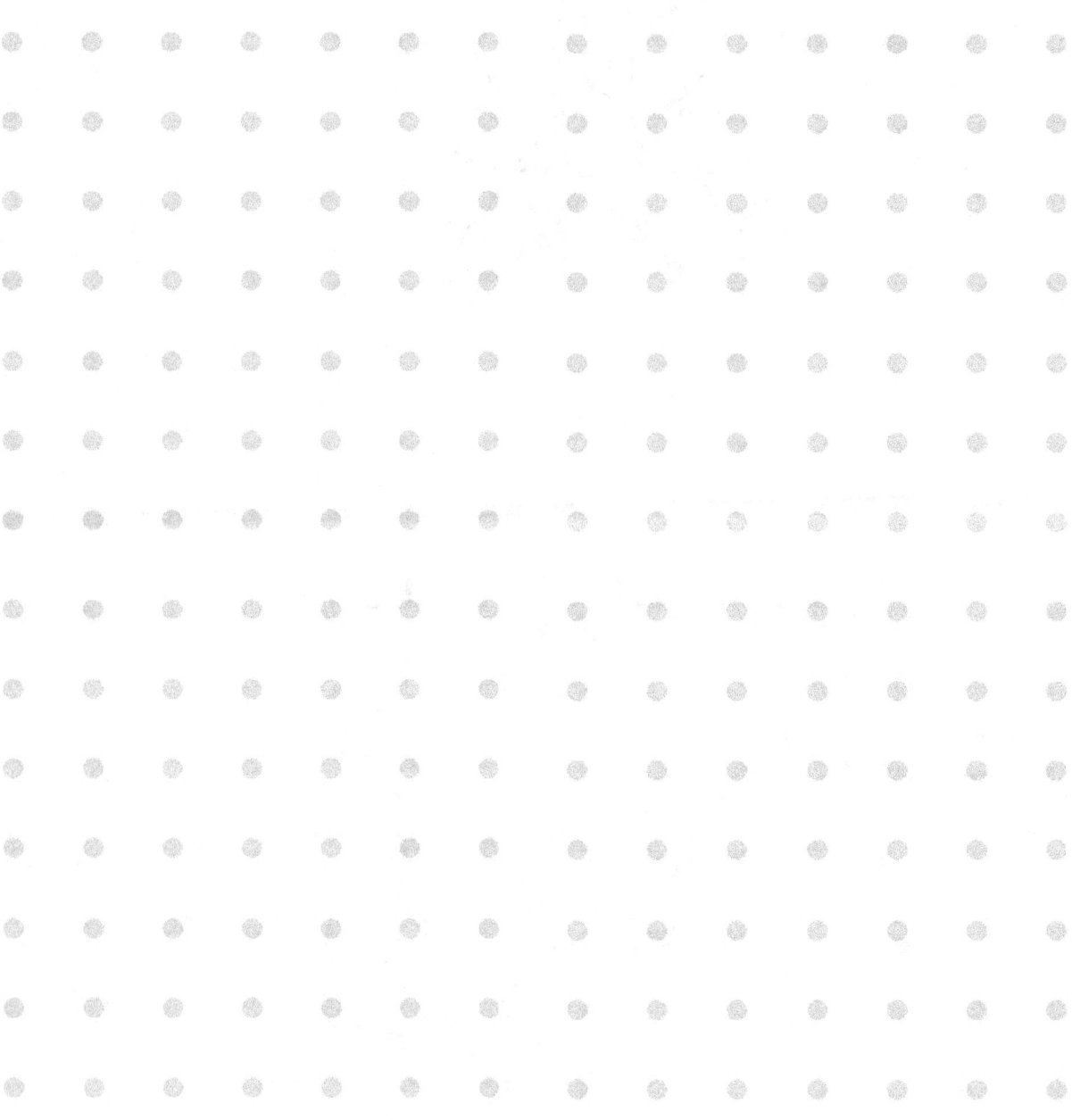

See this

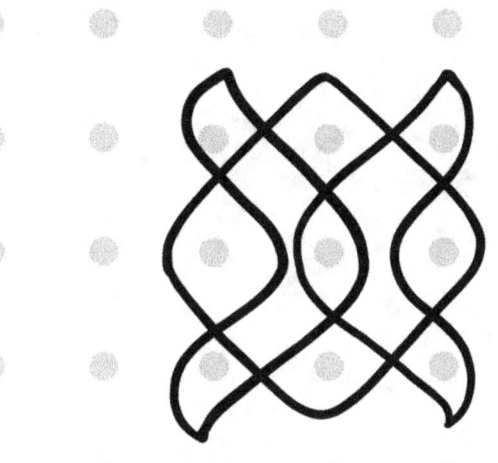

And draw here..

Practice pages

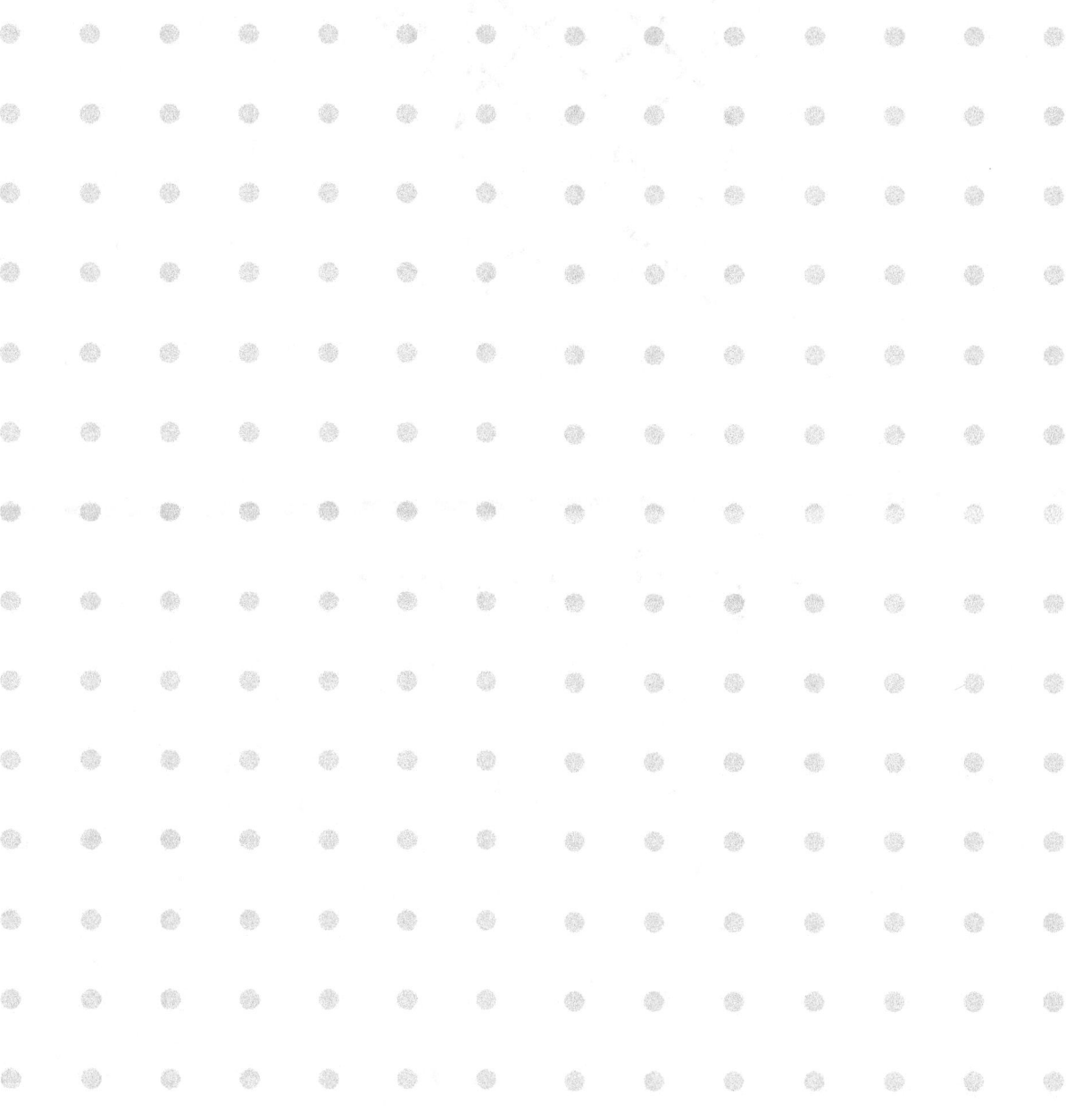

See this

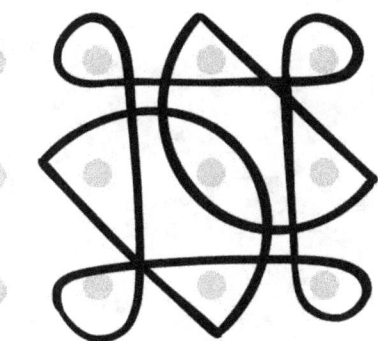

And draw here..

Practice pages

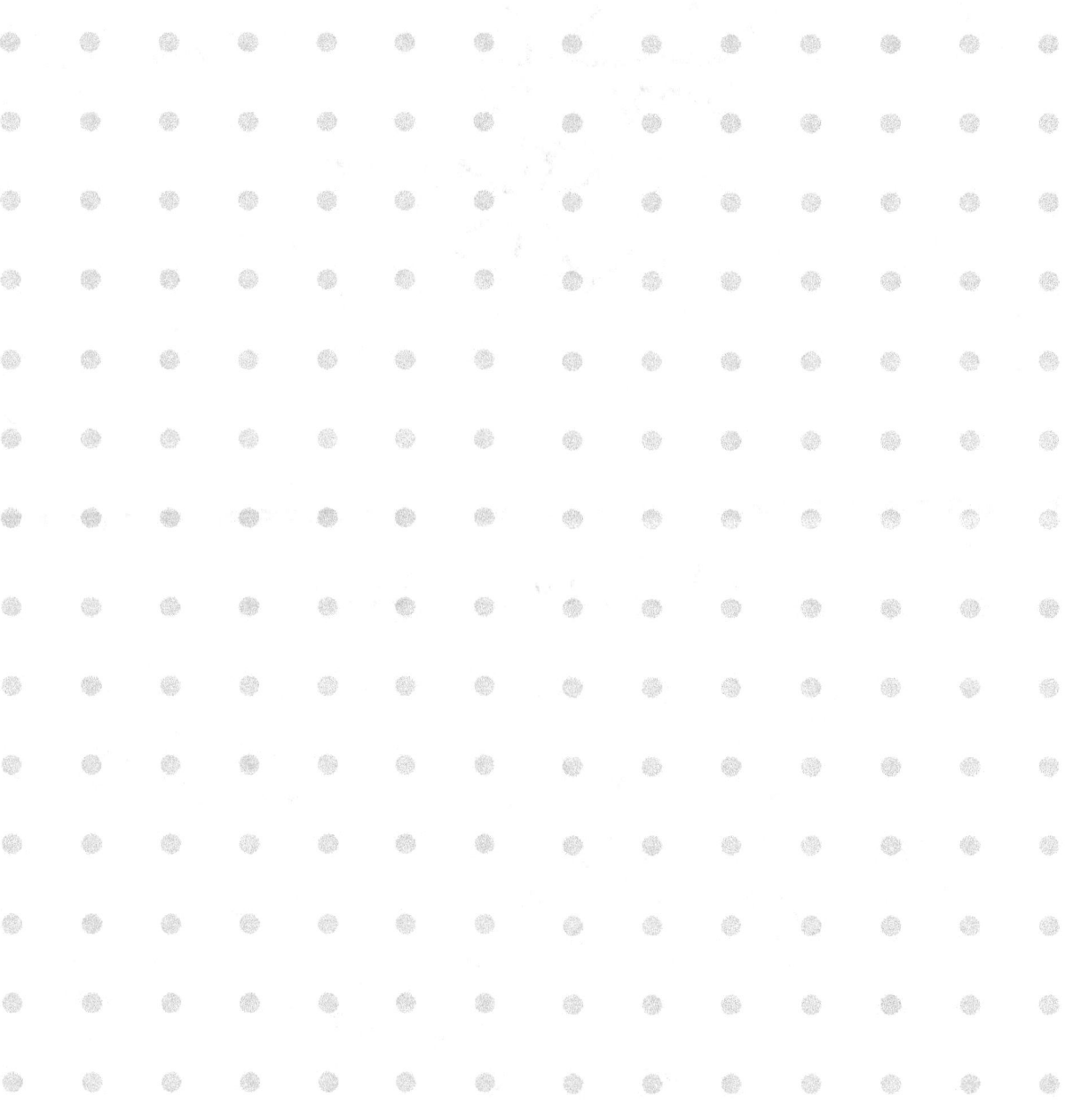

See this

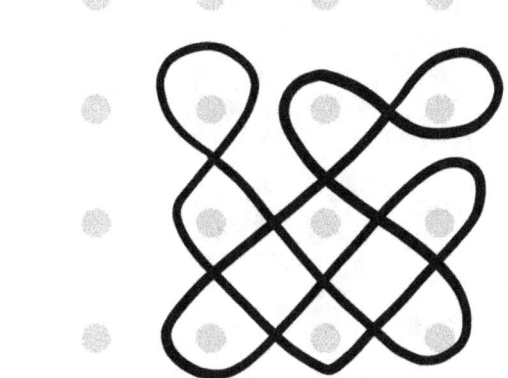

And draw here..

Practice pages

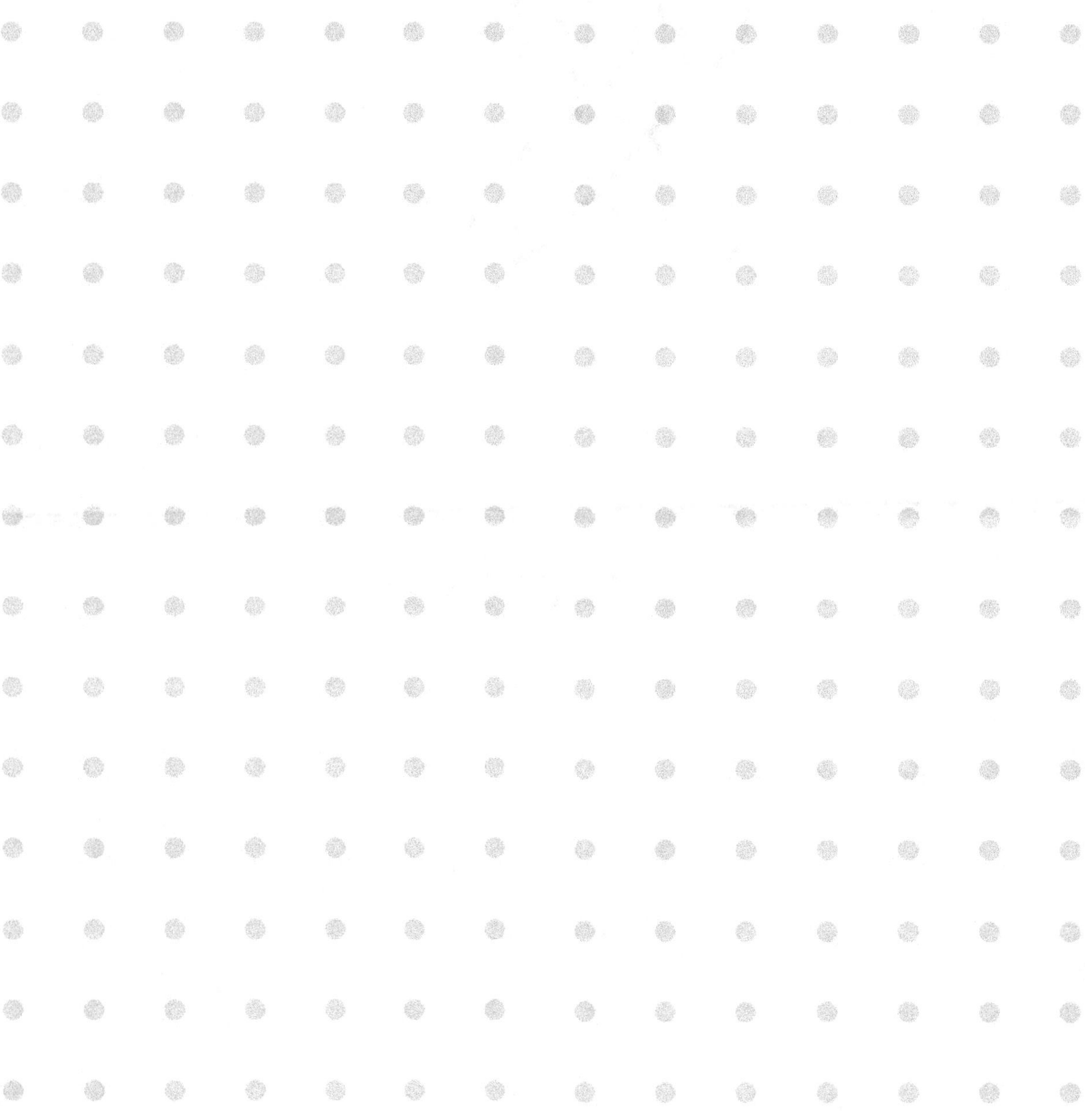

See this

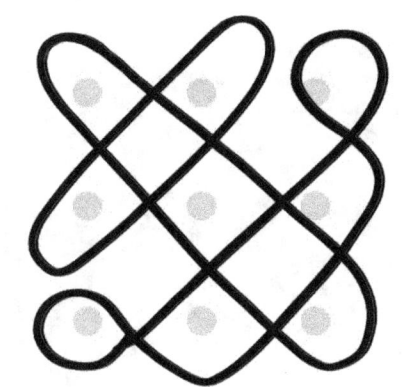

And draw here..

Practice pages

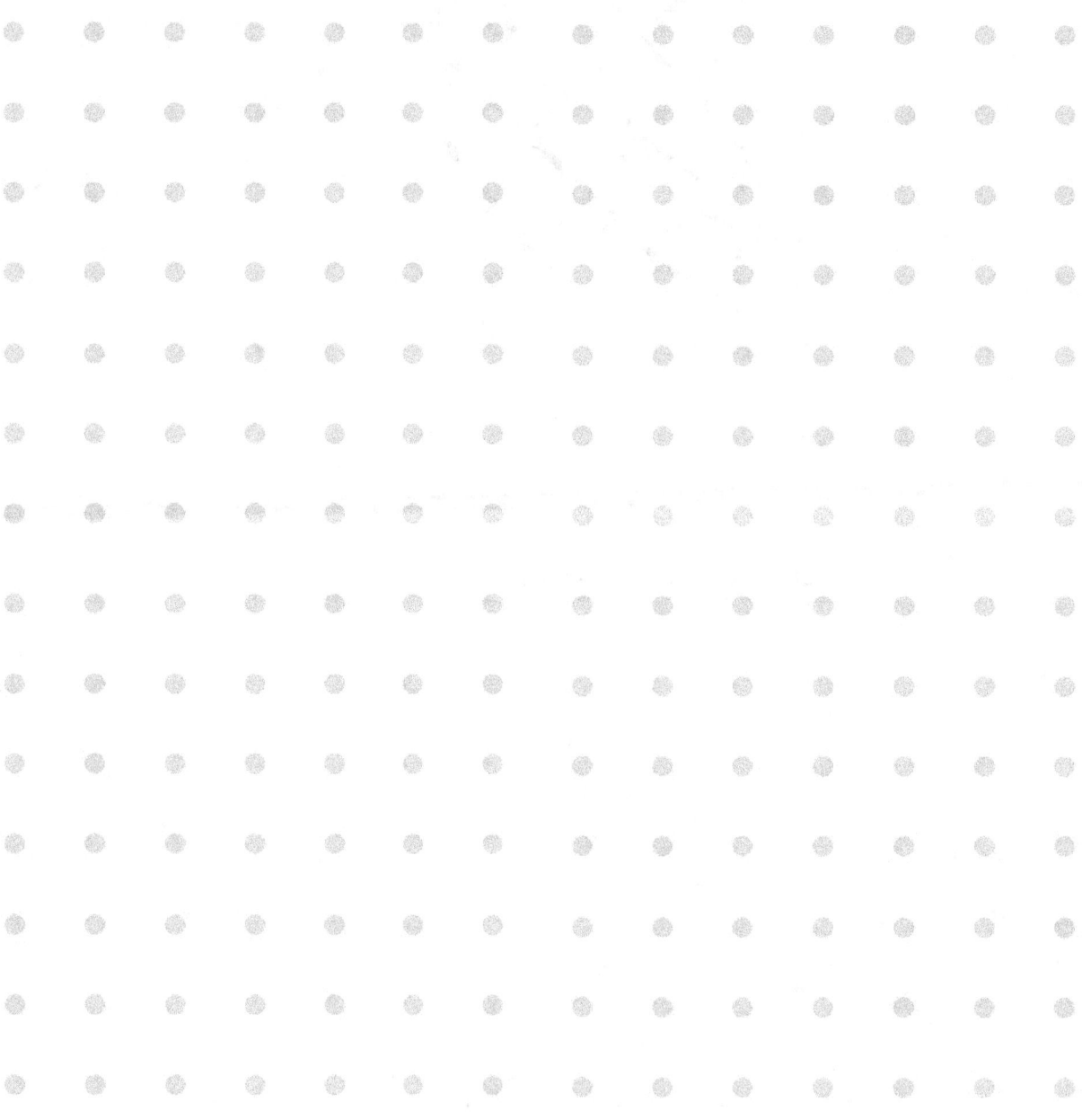

See this

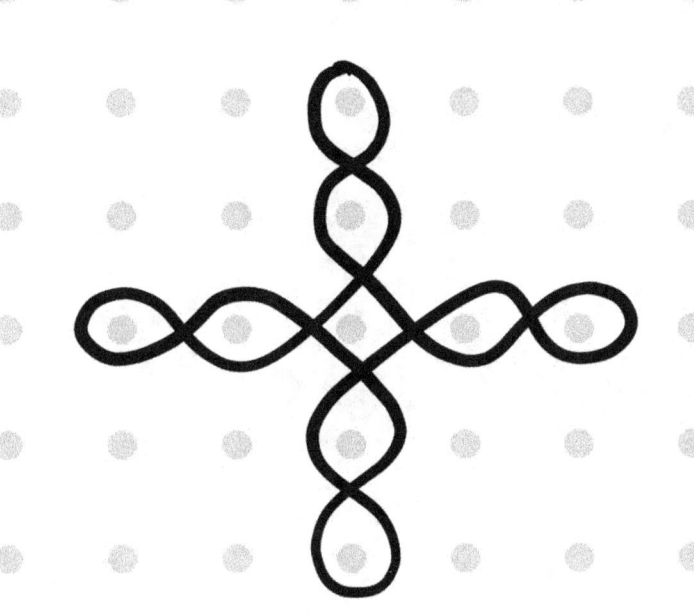

And draw here..

Practice pages

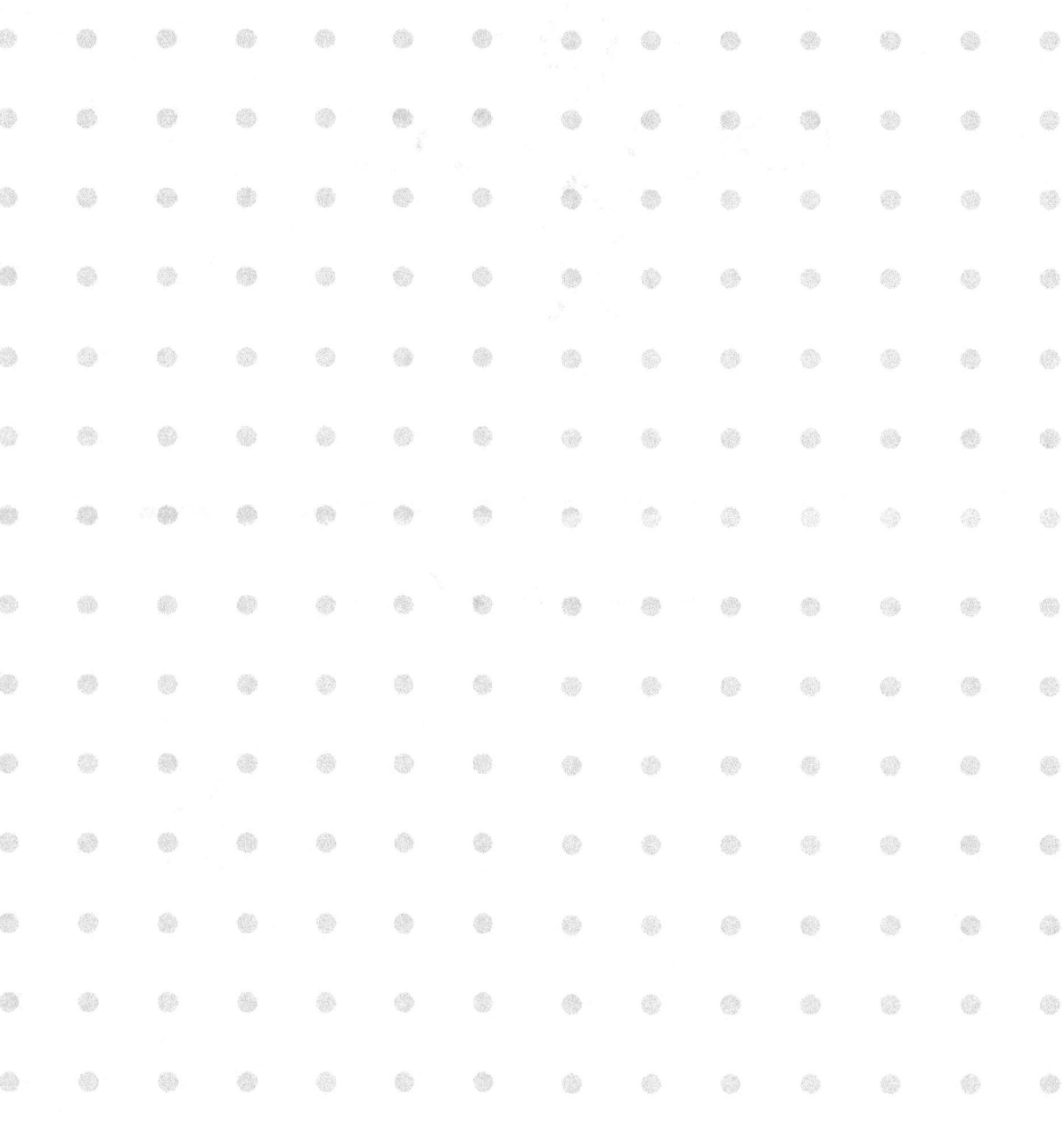

See this

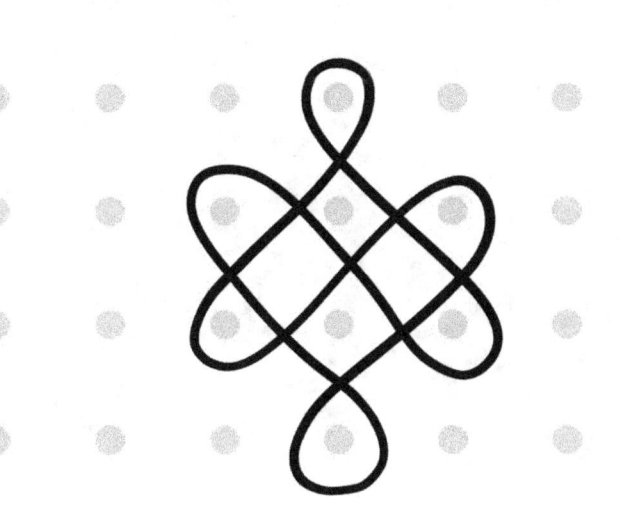

And draw here..

Practice pages

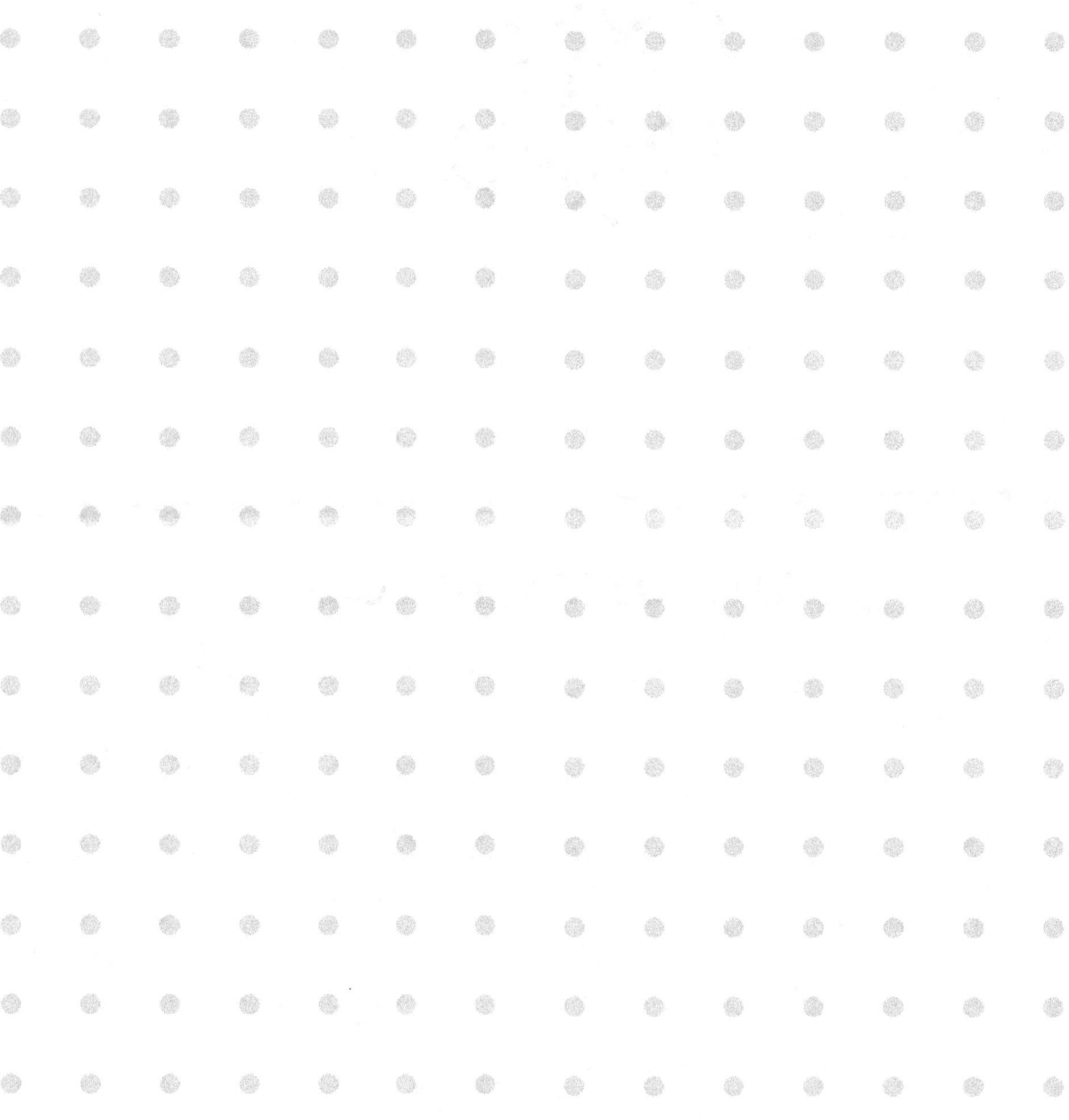

See this

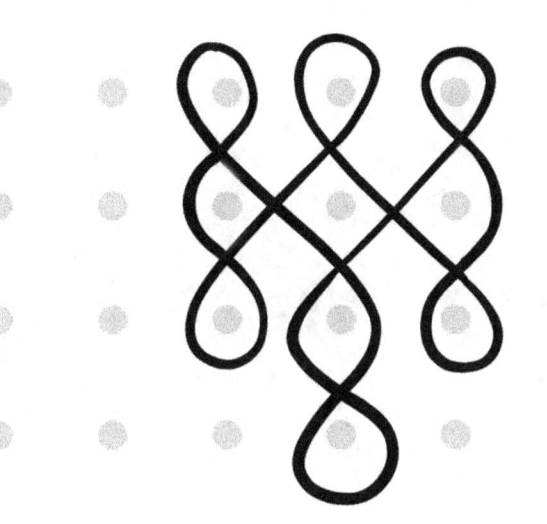

And draw here..

Practice pages

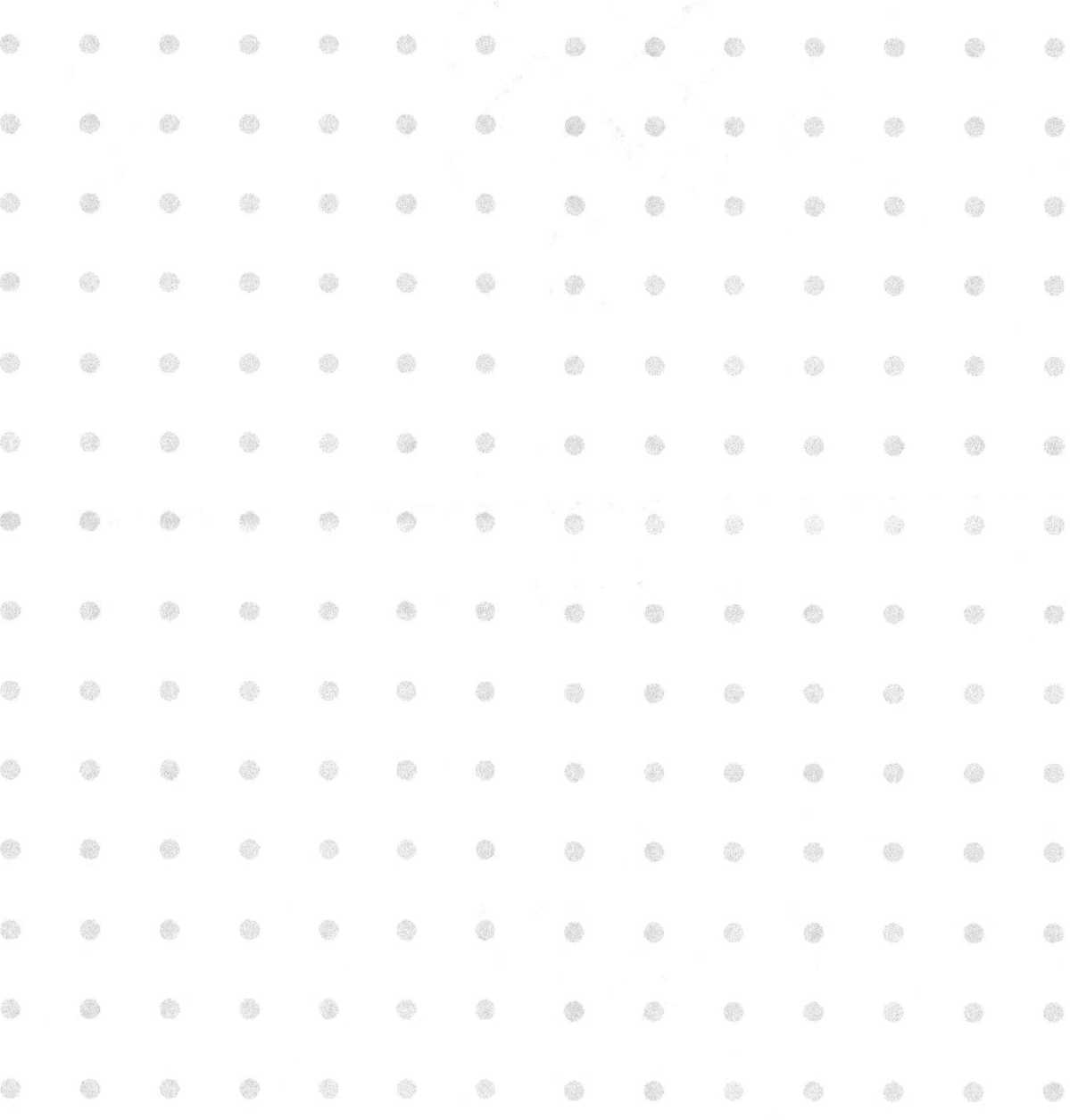

See this

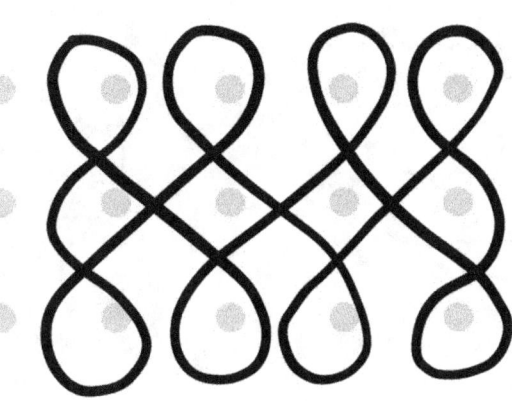

And draw here..

Practice pages

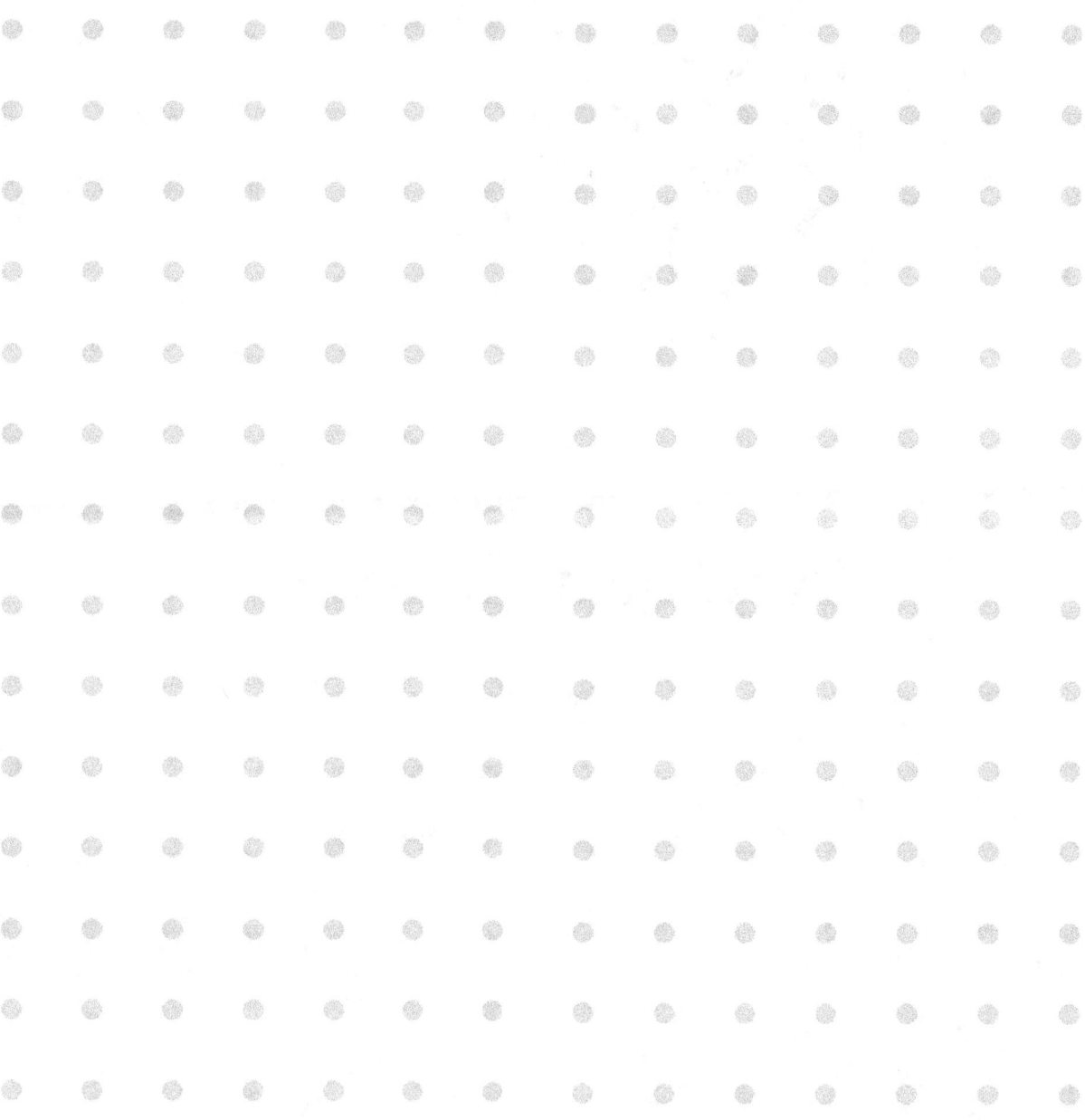

See this

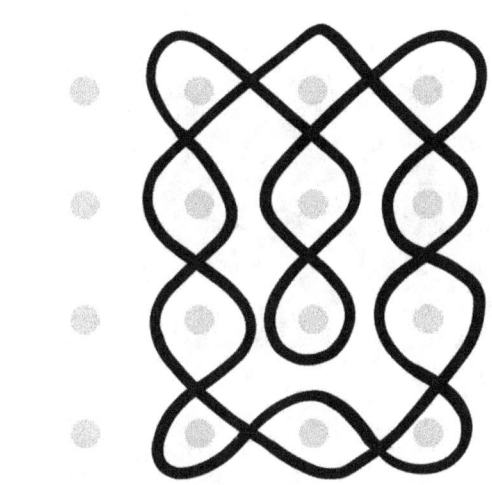

And draw here..

Practice pages

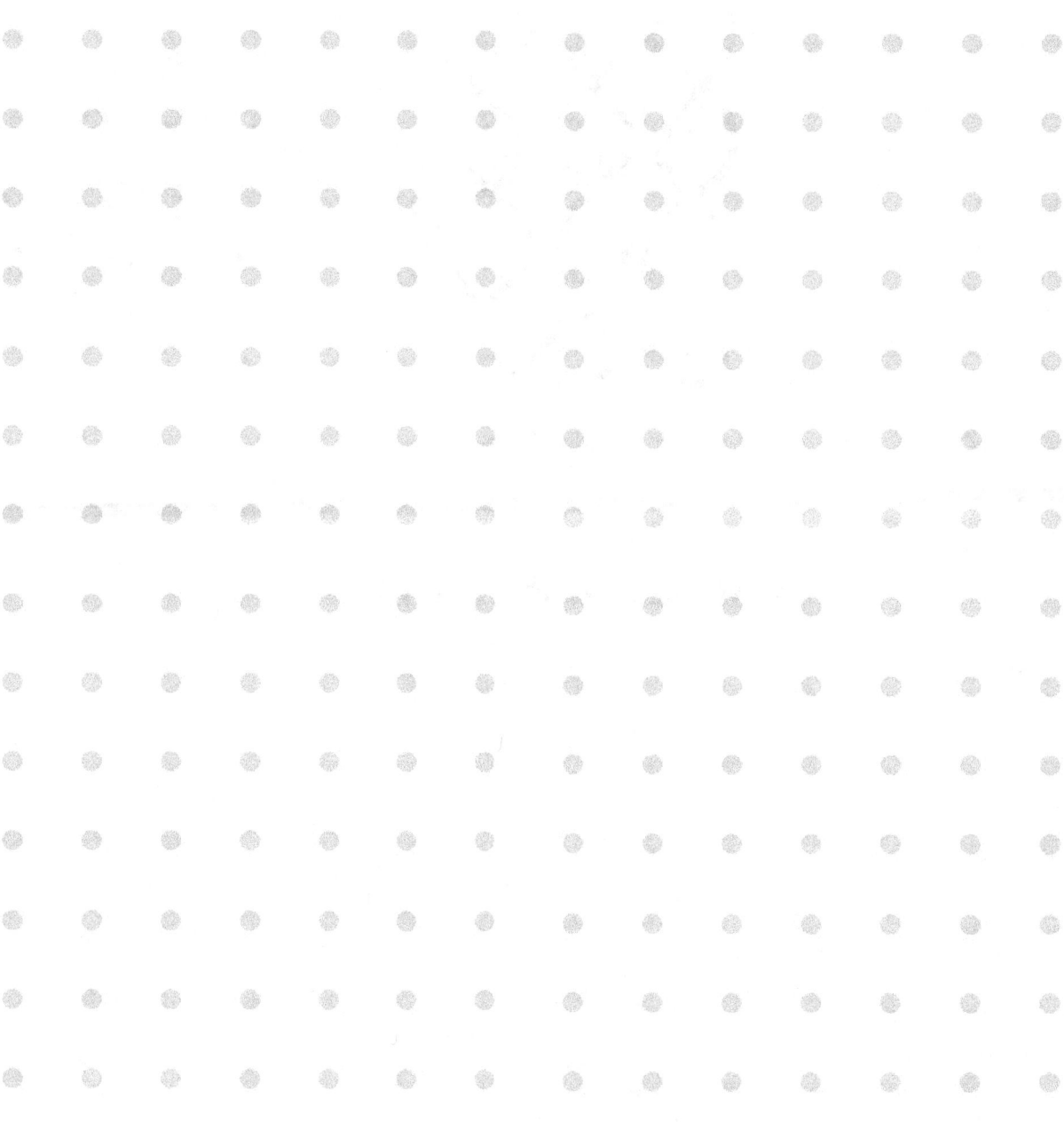

See this

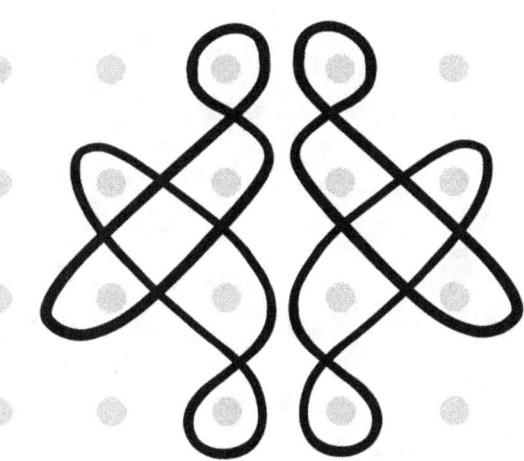

And draw here..

Practice pages

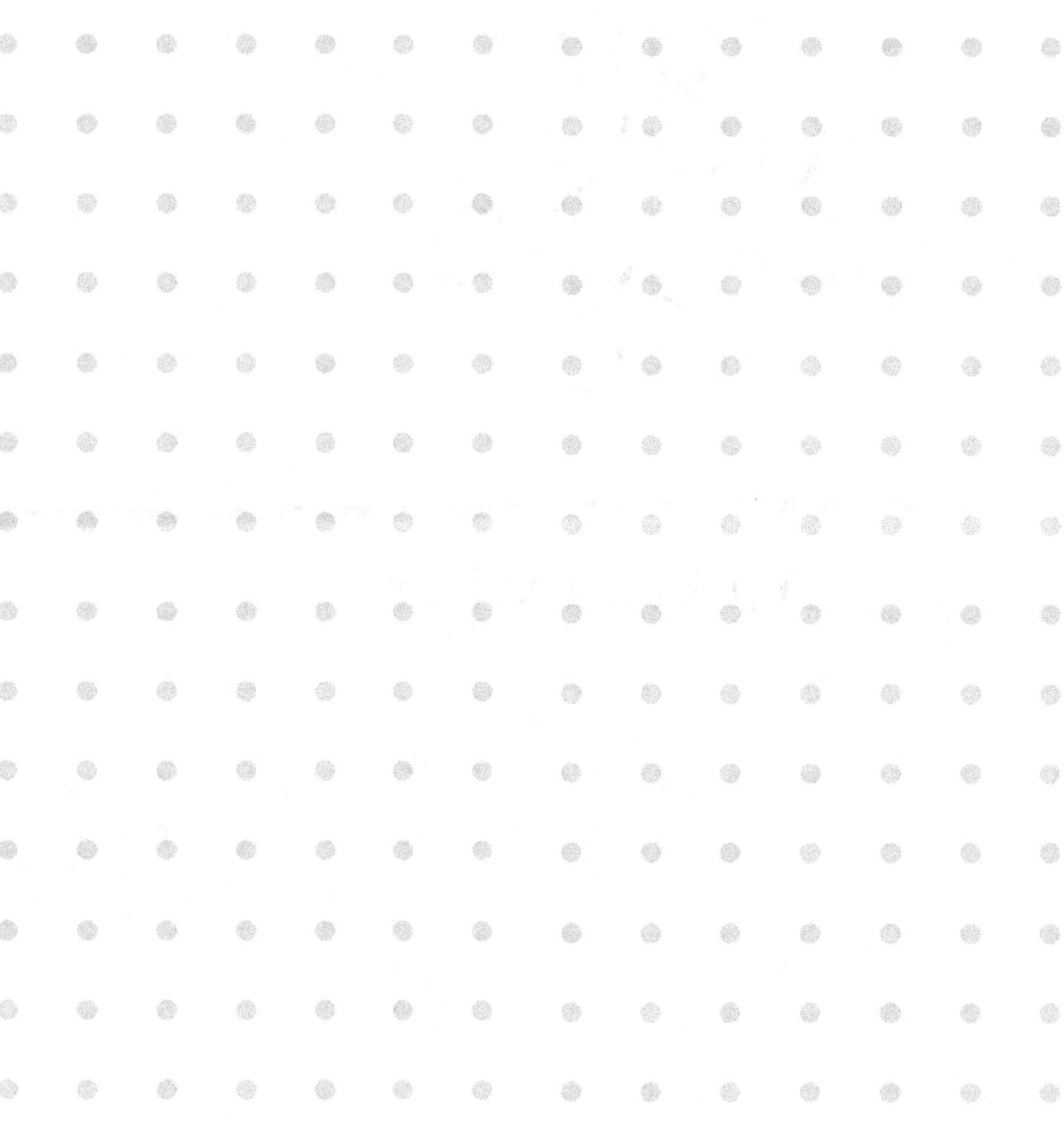

See this

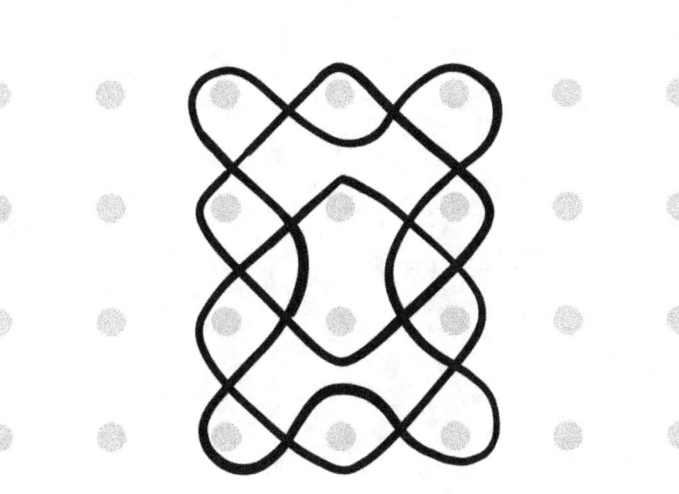

And draw here..

Practice pages

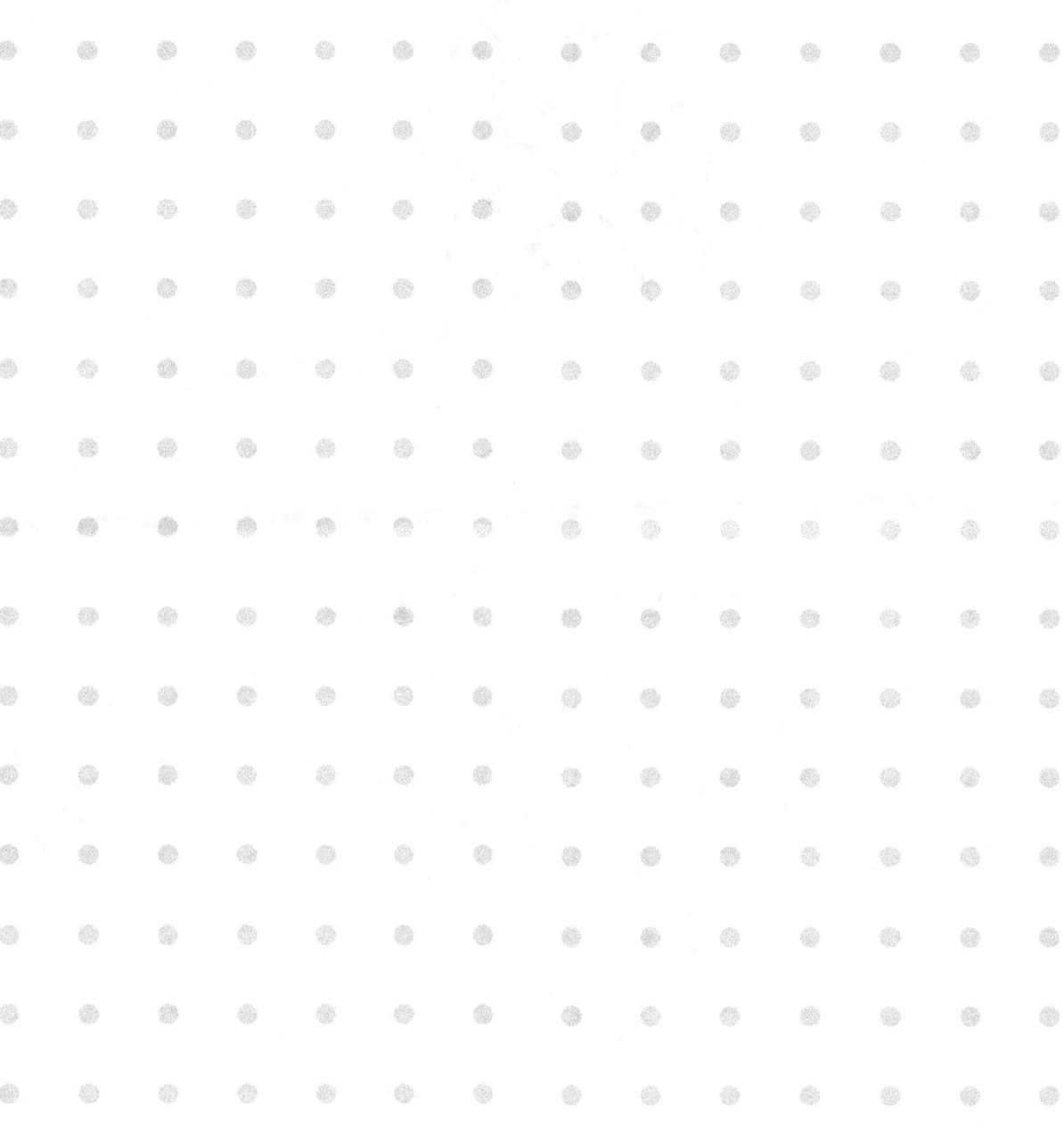

See this

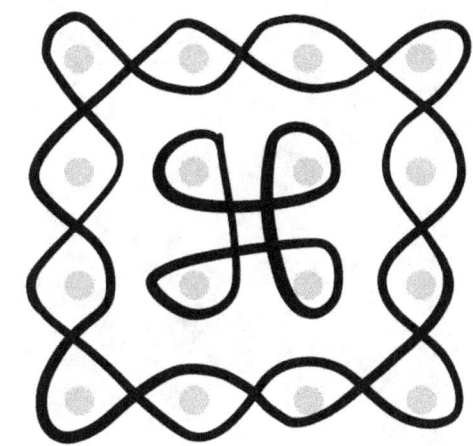

And draw here..

Practice pages

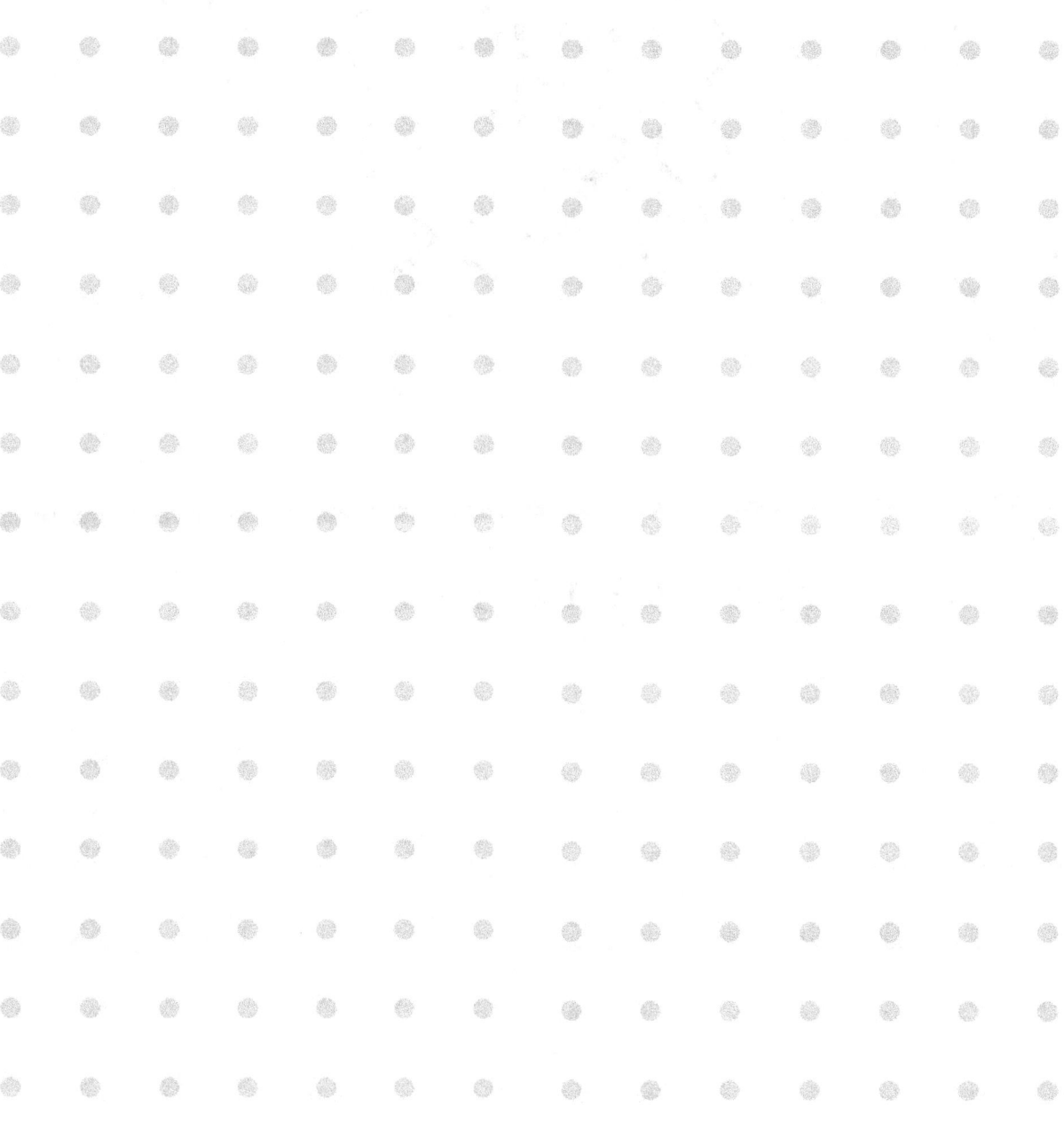

See this

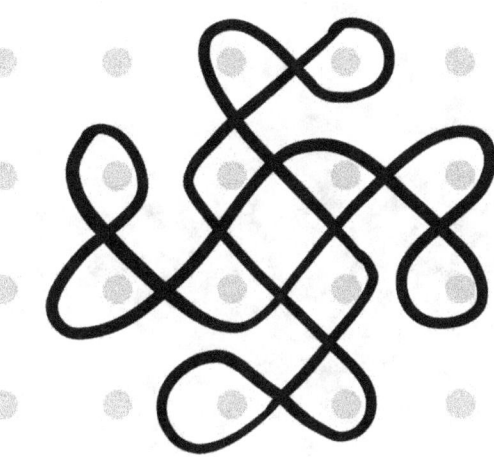

And draw here..

Practice pages

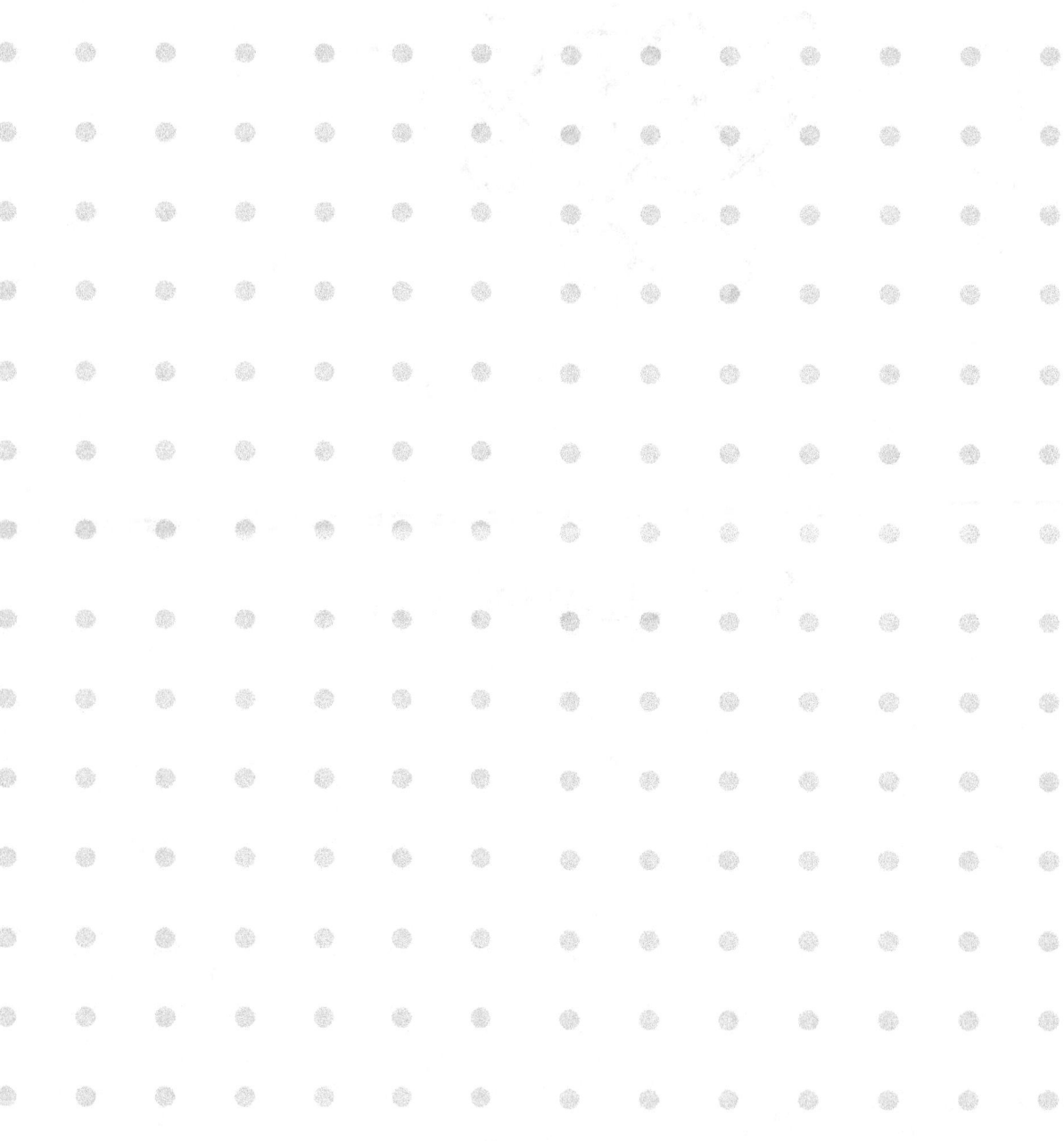

See this

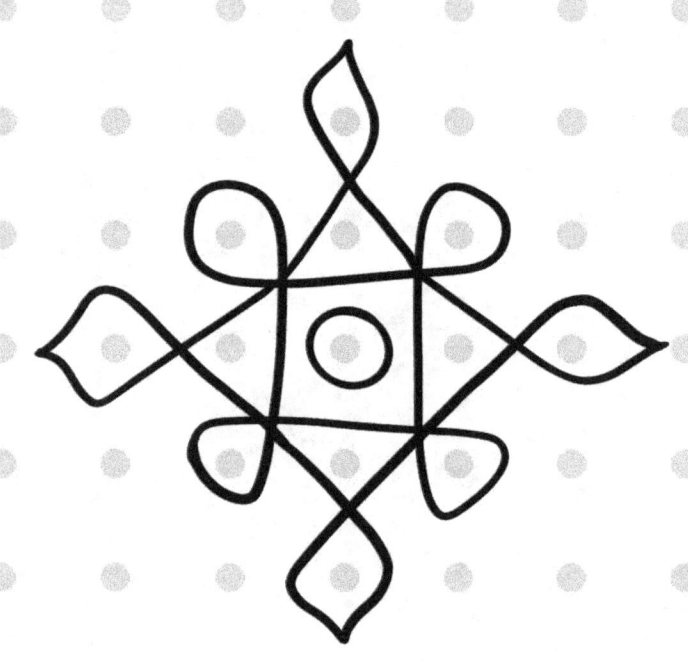

And draw here..

Practice pages

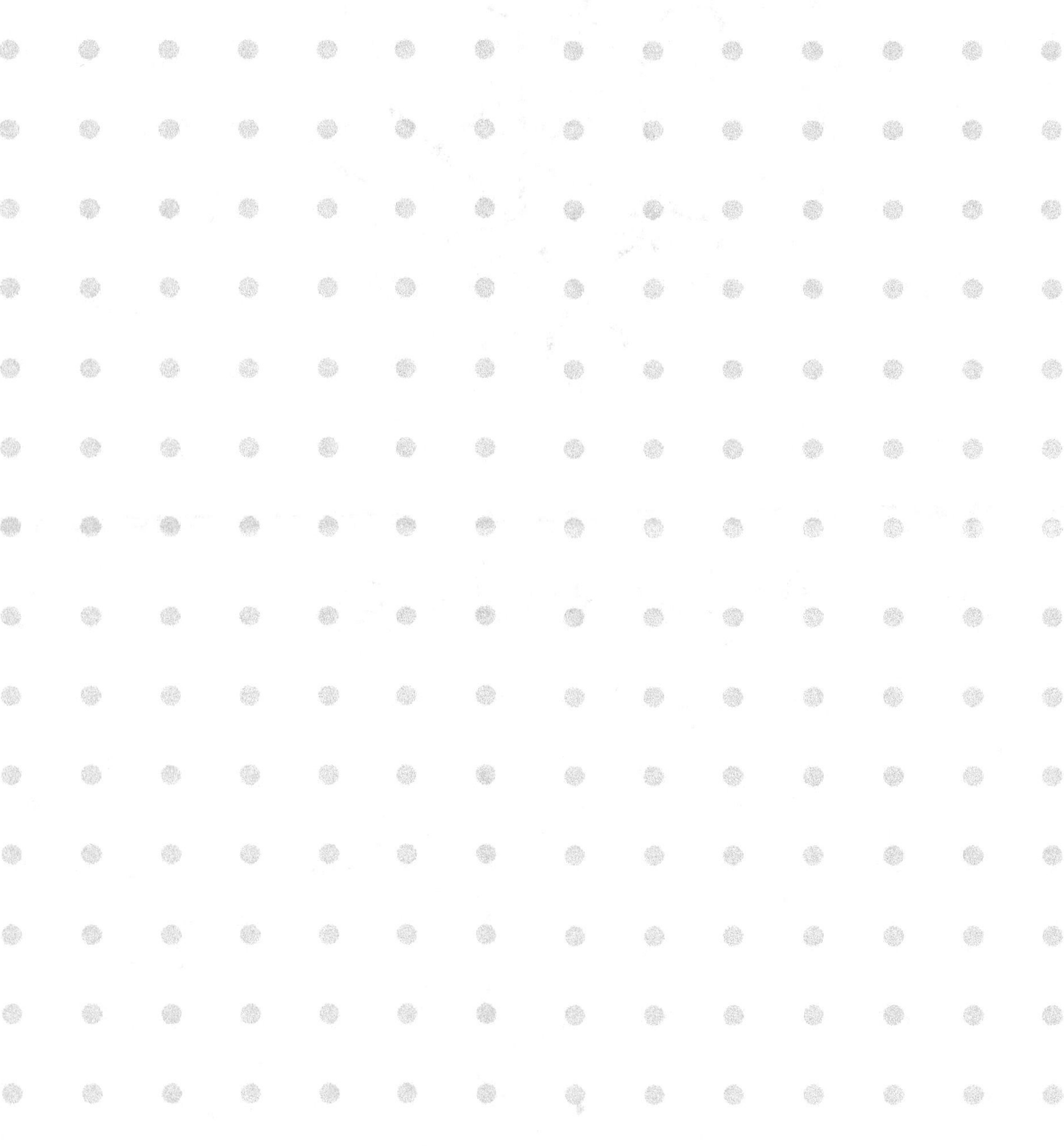

See this

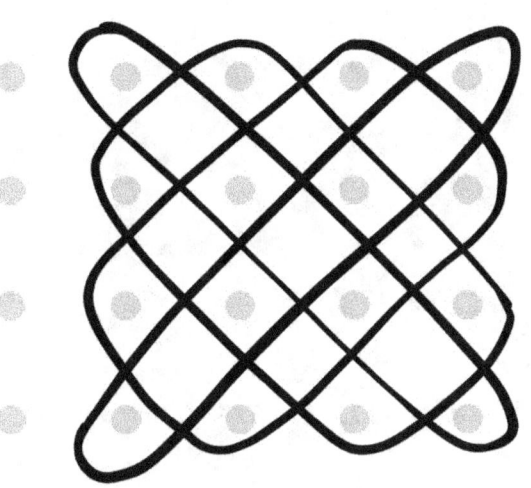

And draw here..

Practice pages

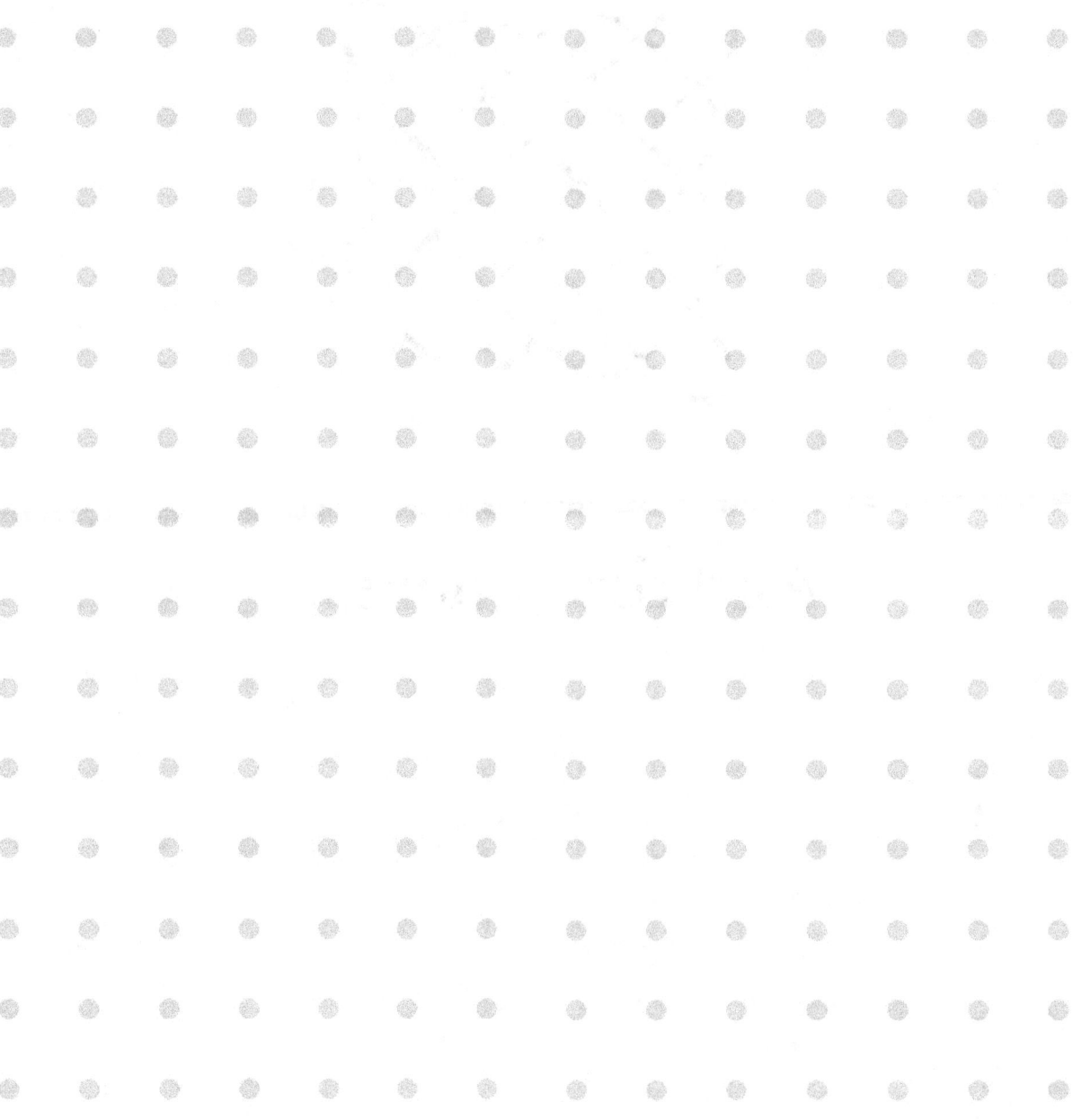

See this

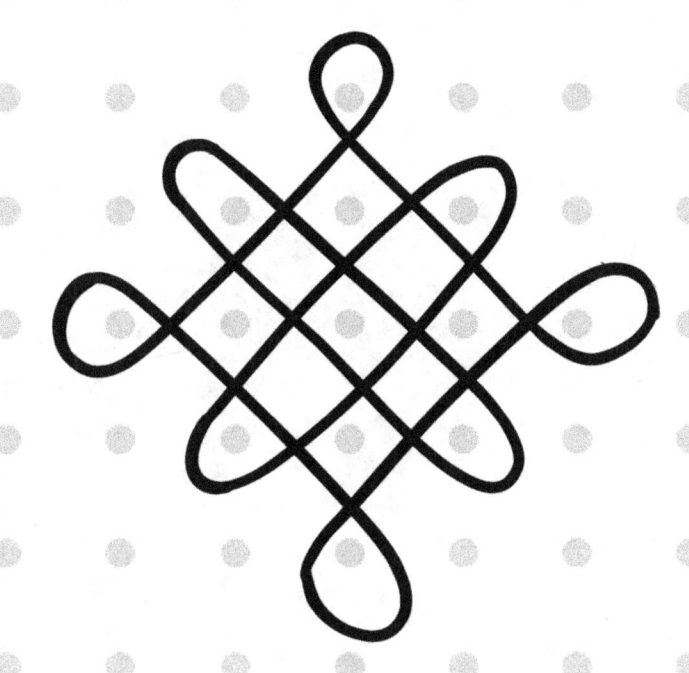

And draw here..

Practice pages

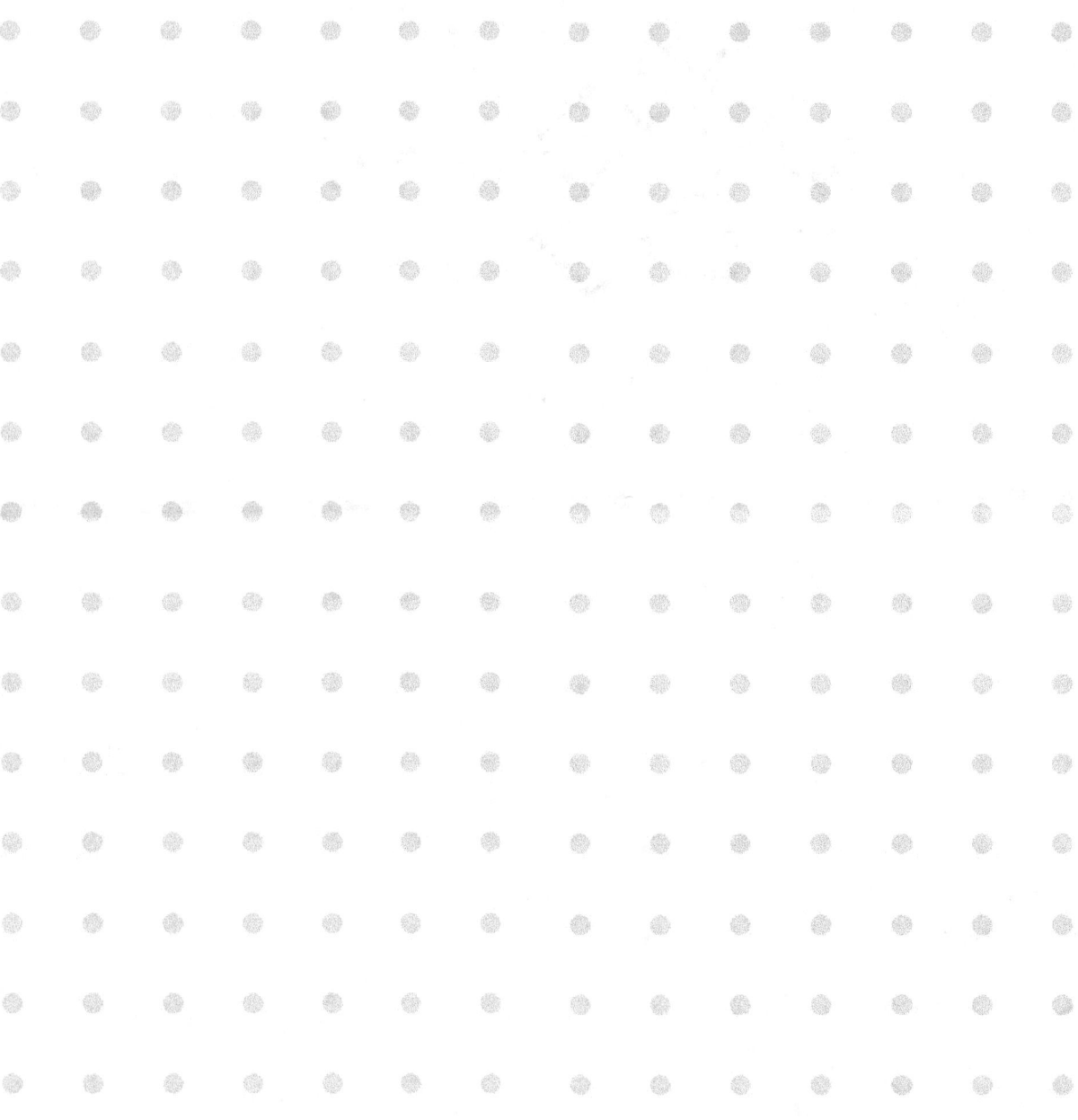

See this

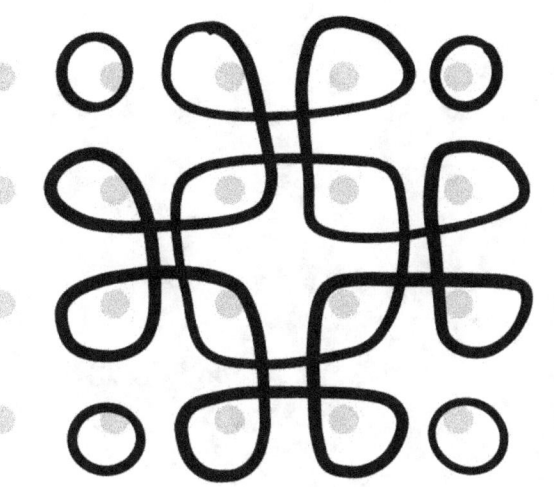

And draw here..

Practice pages

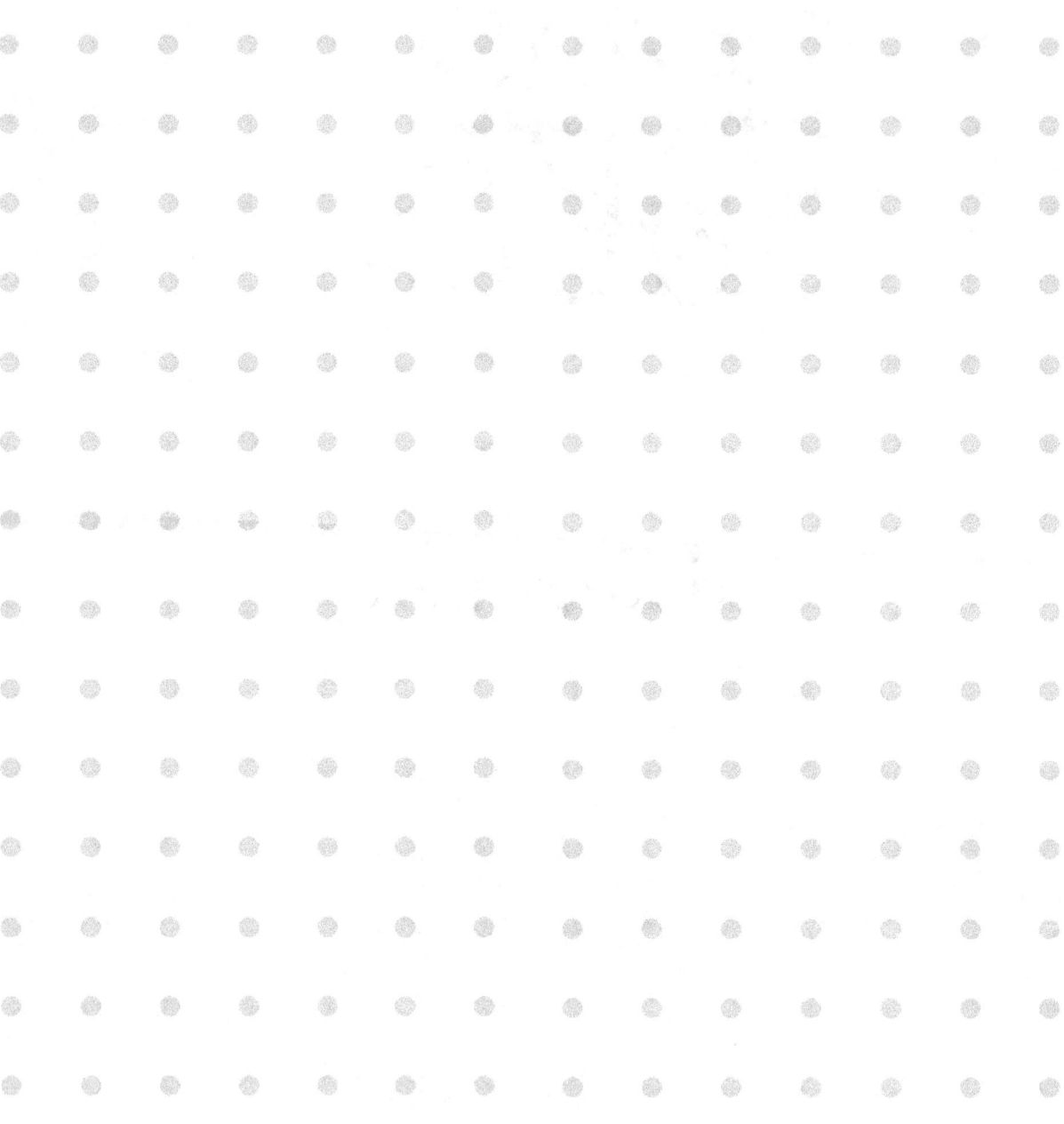

See this

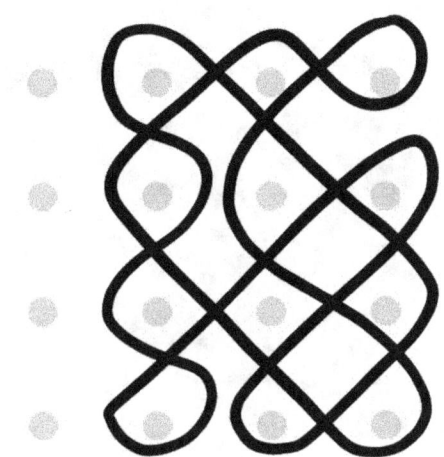

And draw here..

Practice pages

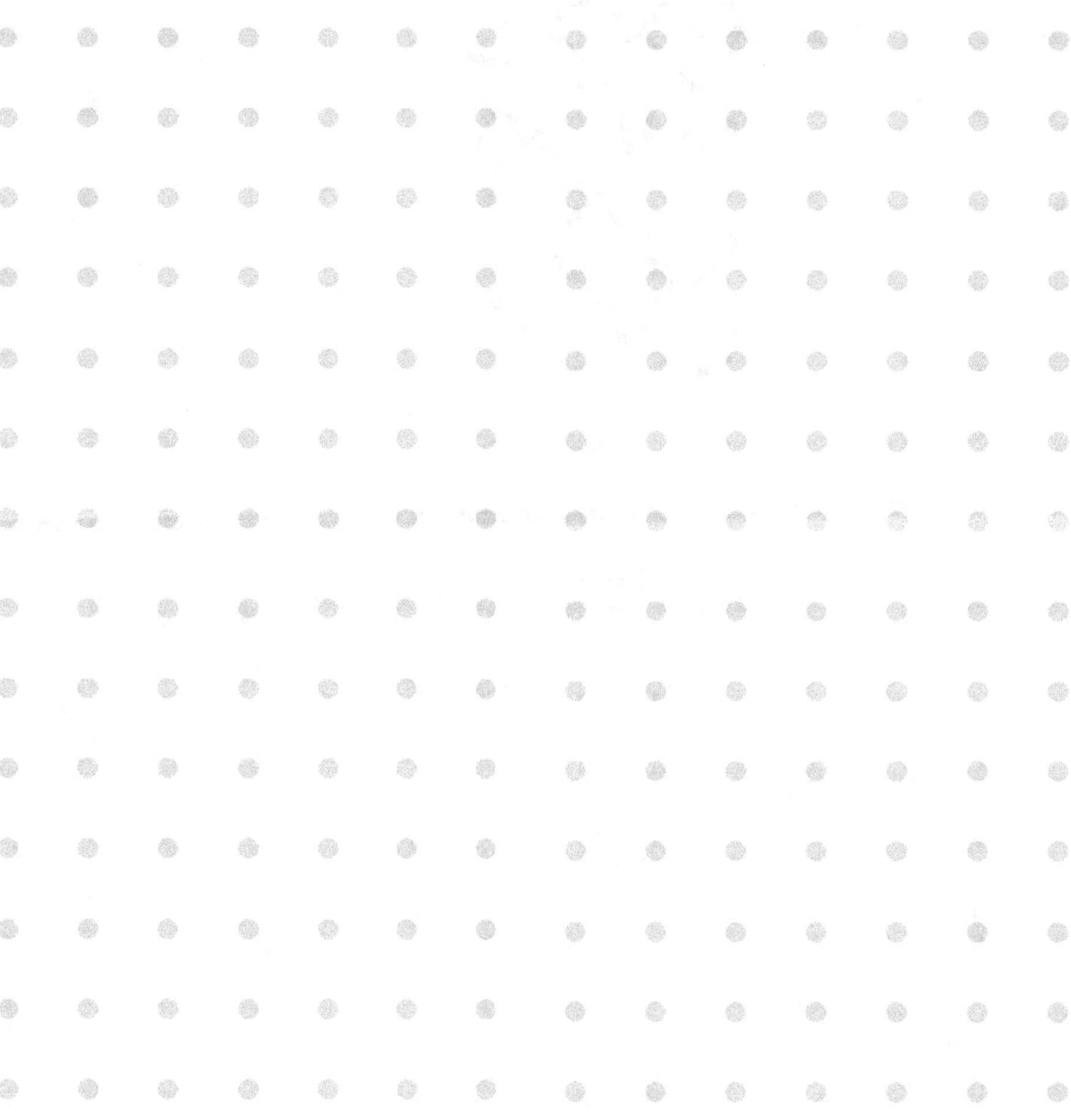

See this

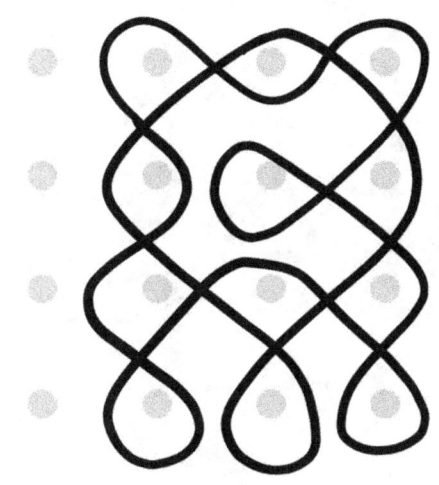

And draw here..

Practice pages

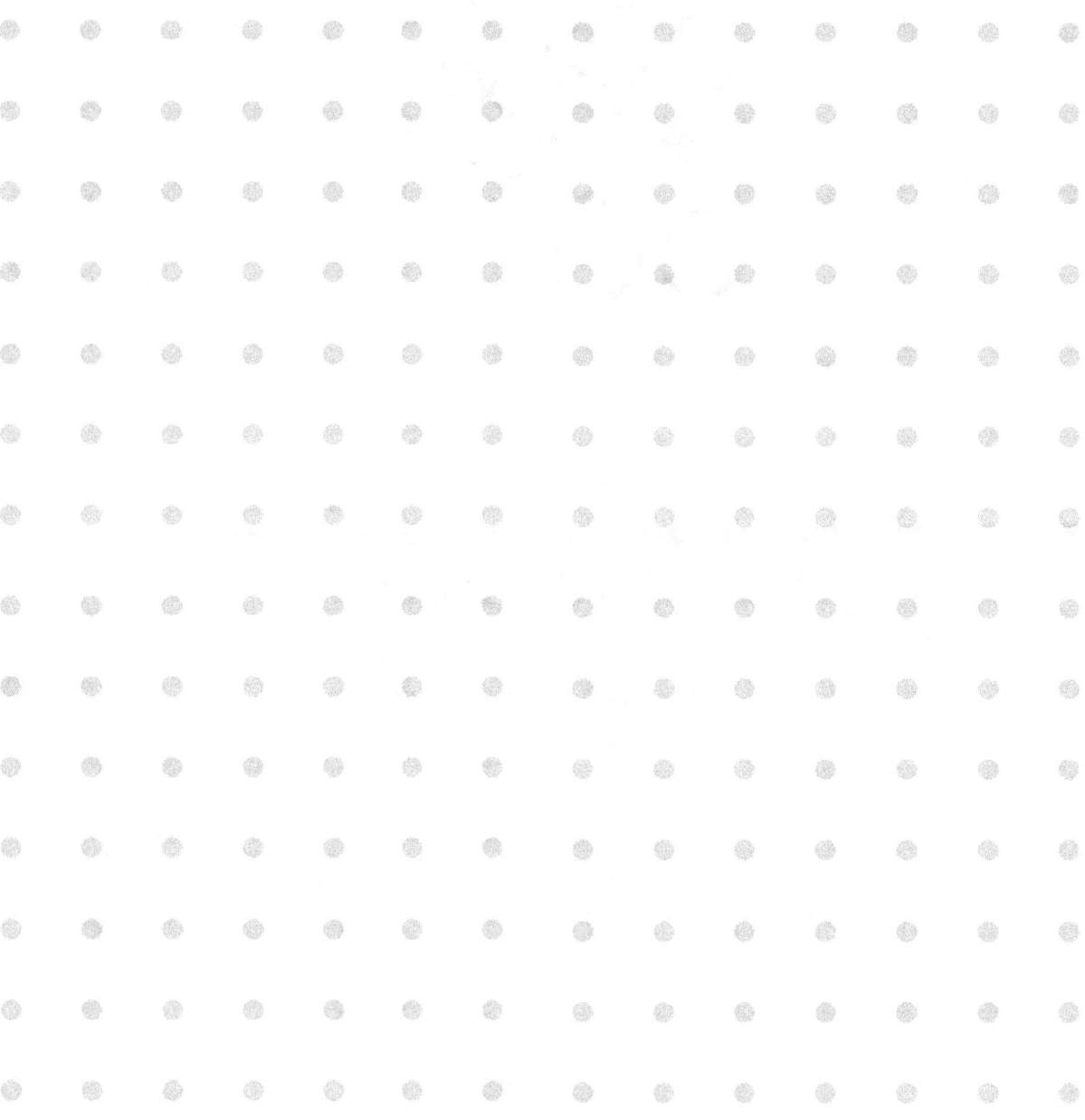

See this

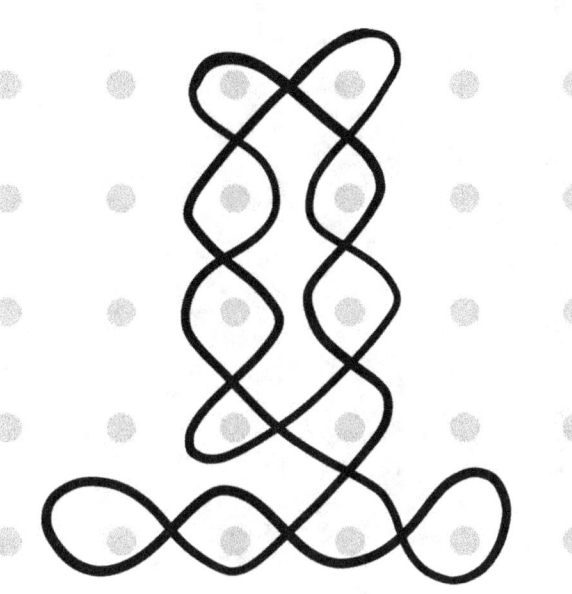

And draw here..

Practice pages

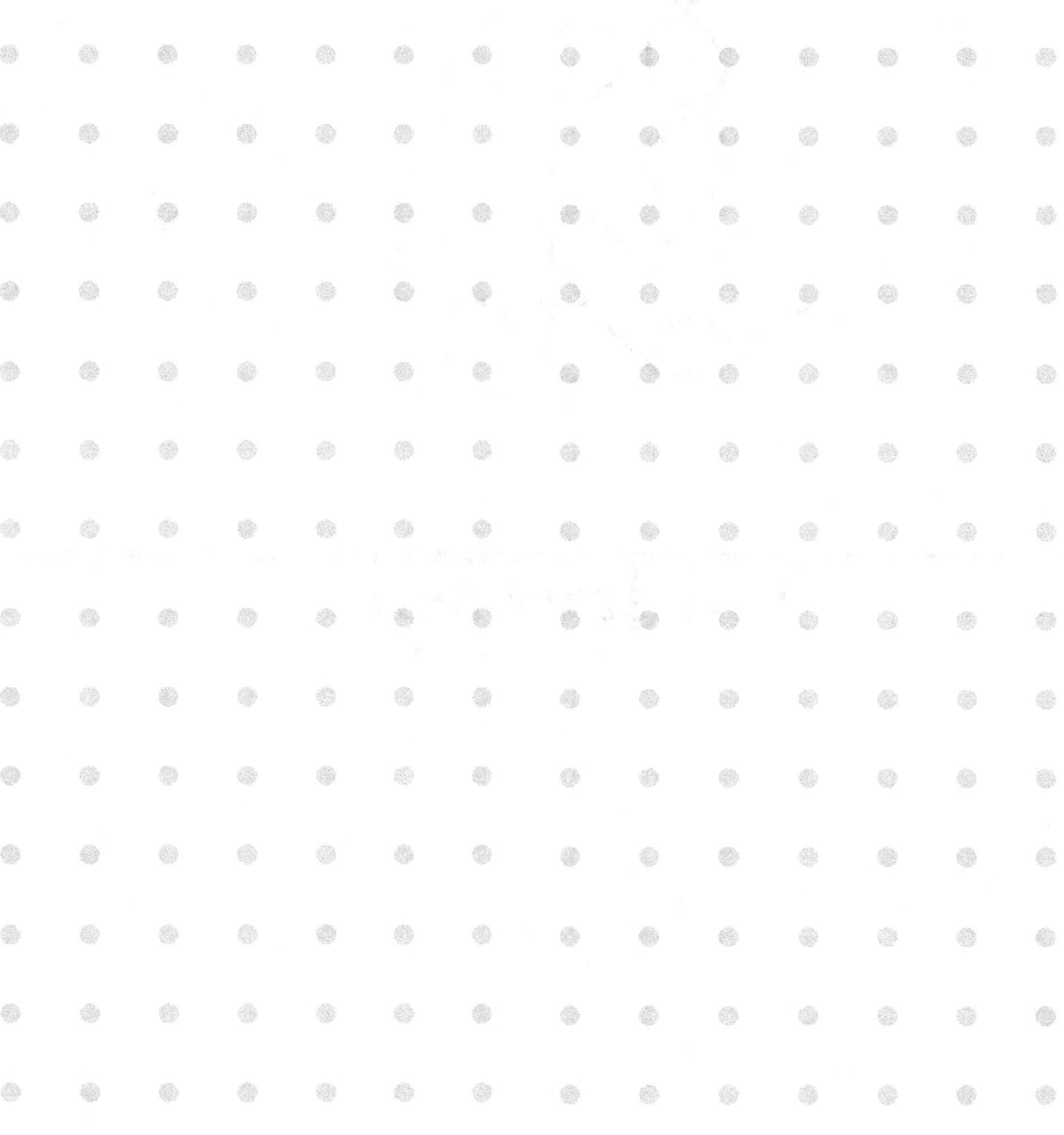

See this

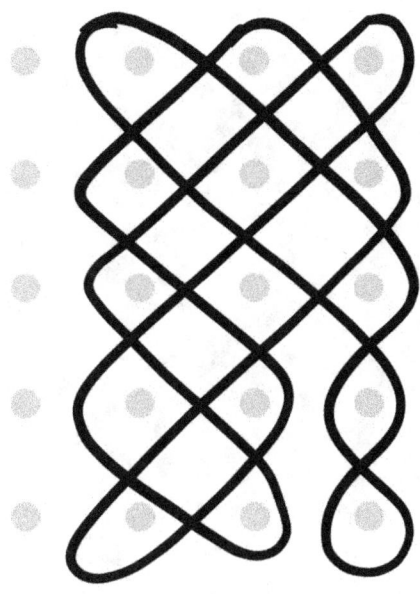

And draw here..

Practice pages

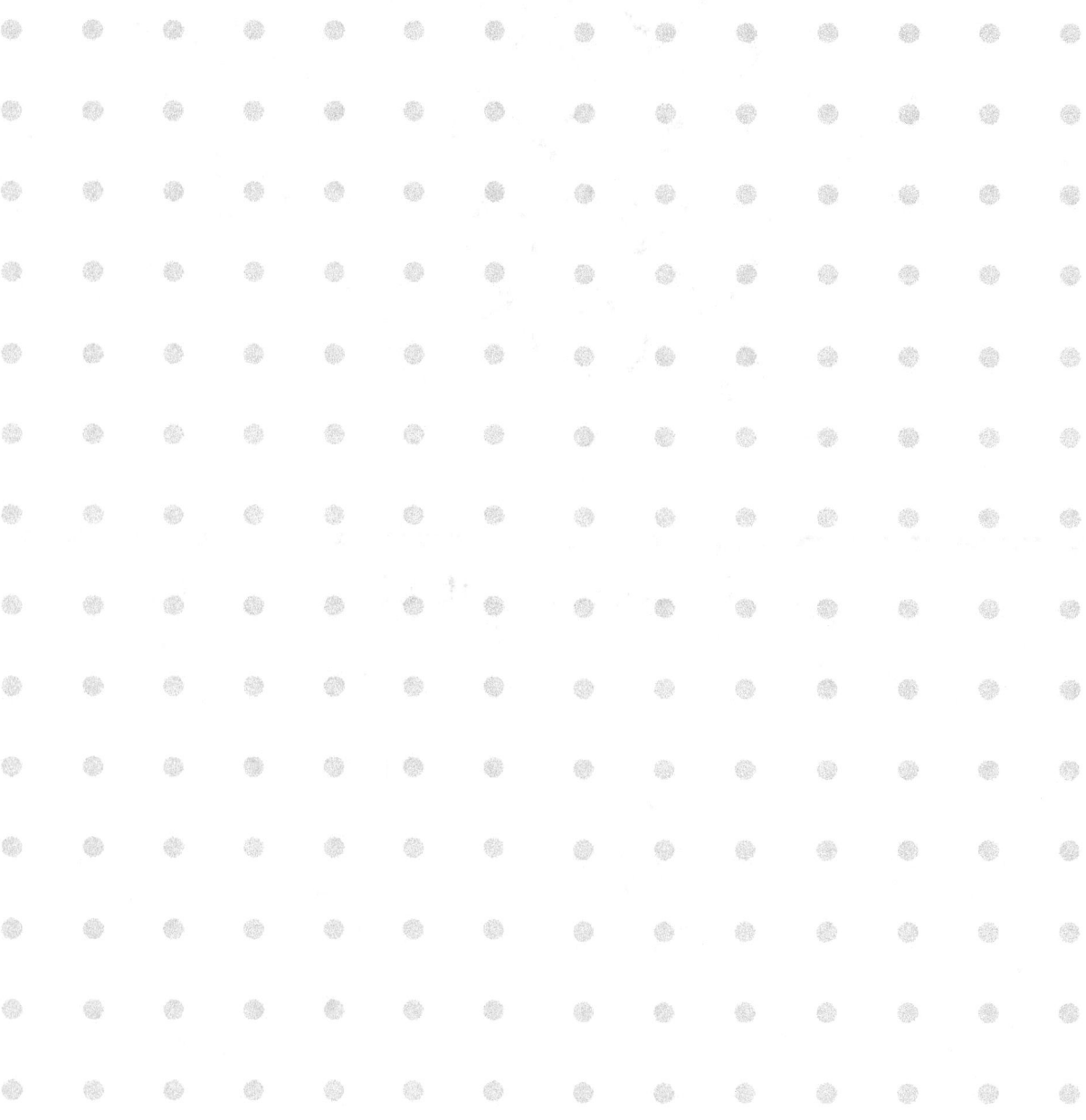

See this

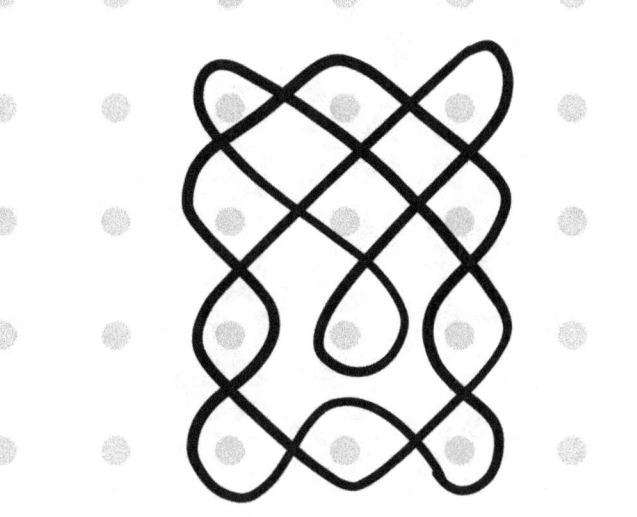

And draw here..

Practice pages

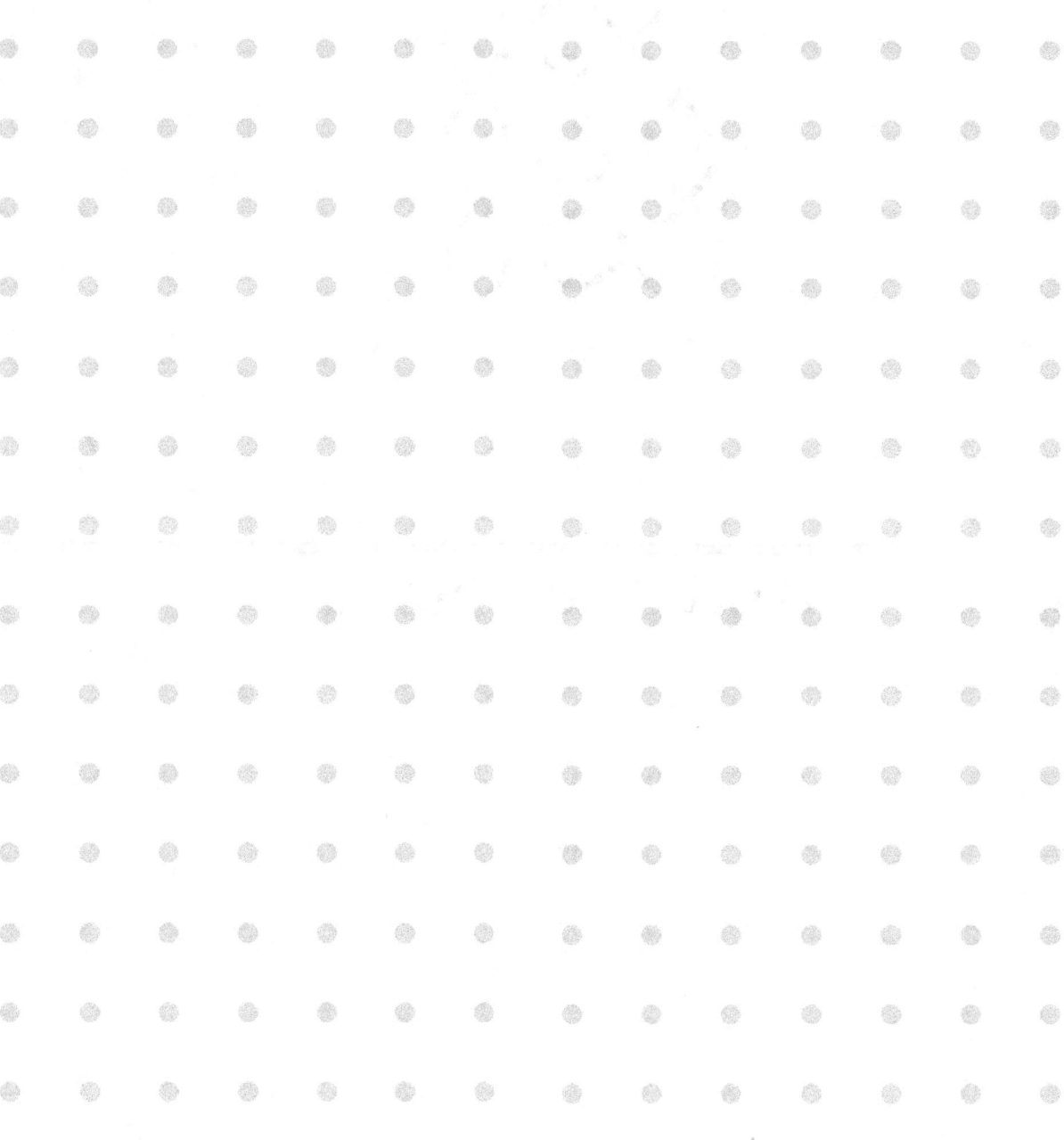

See this

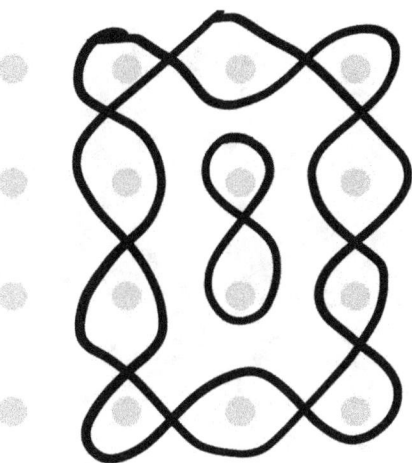

And draw here..

Practice pages

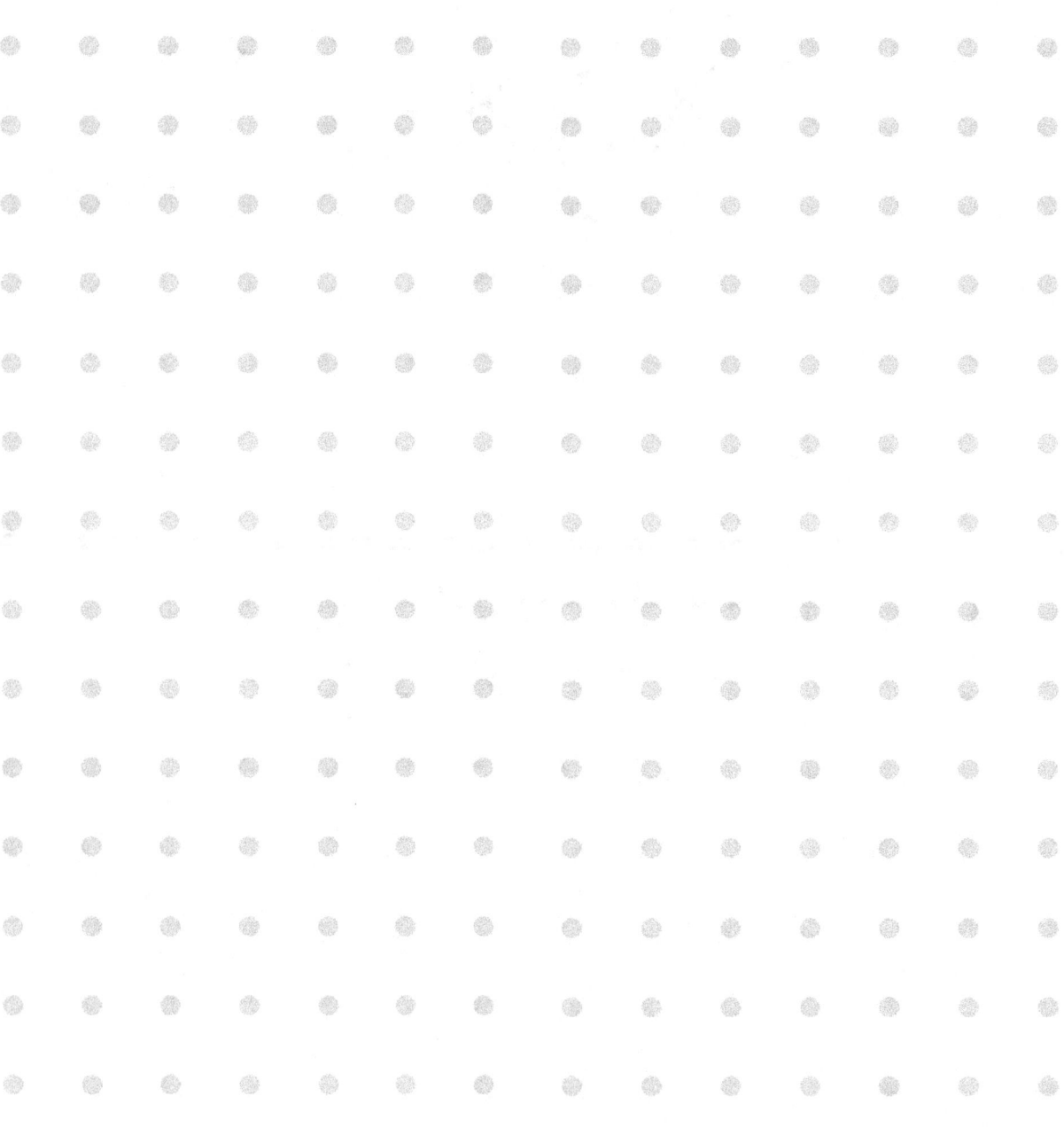

See this

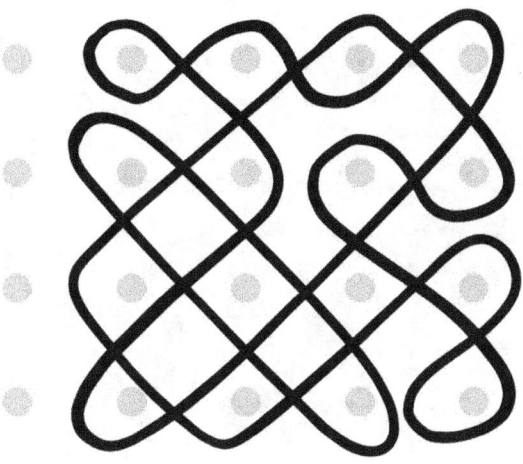

And draw here..

Practice pages

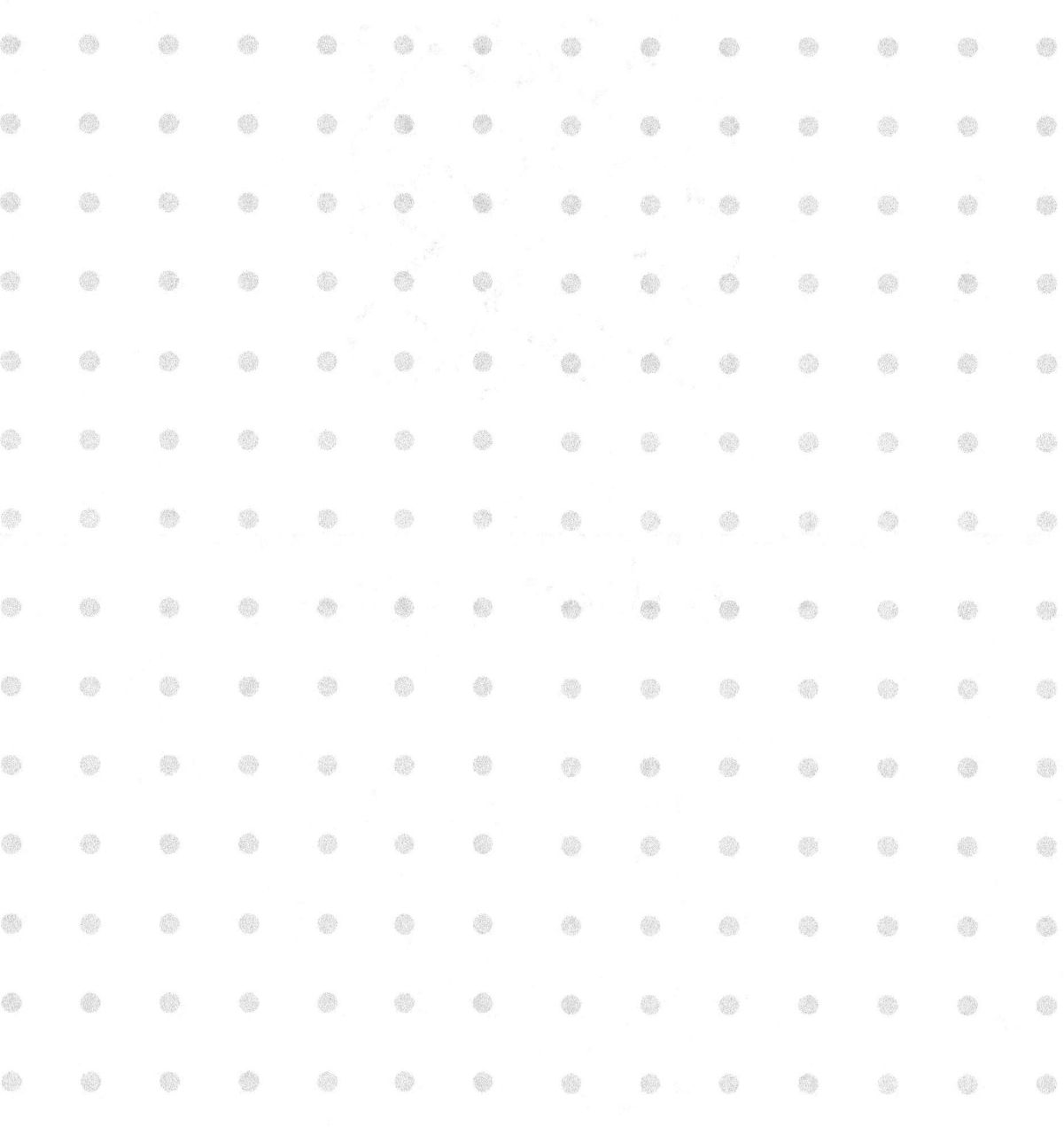

See this

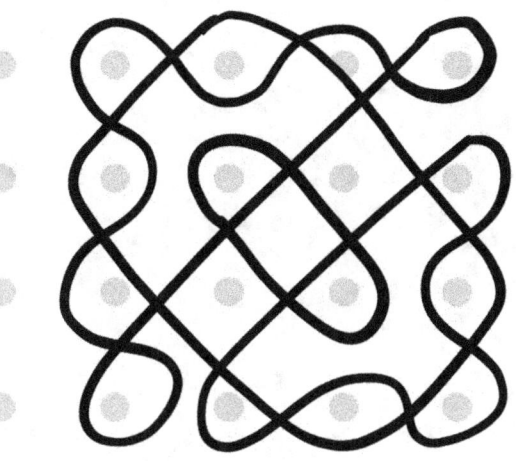

And draw here..

Practice pages

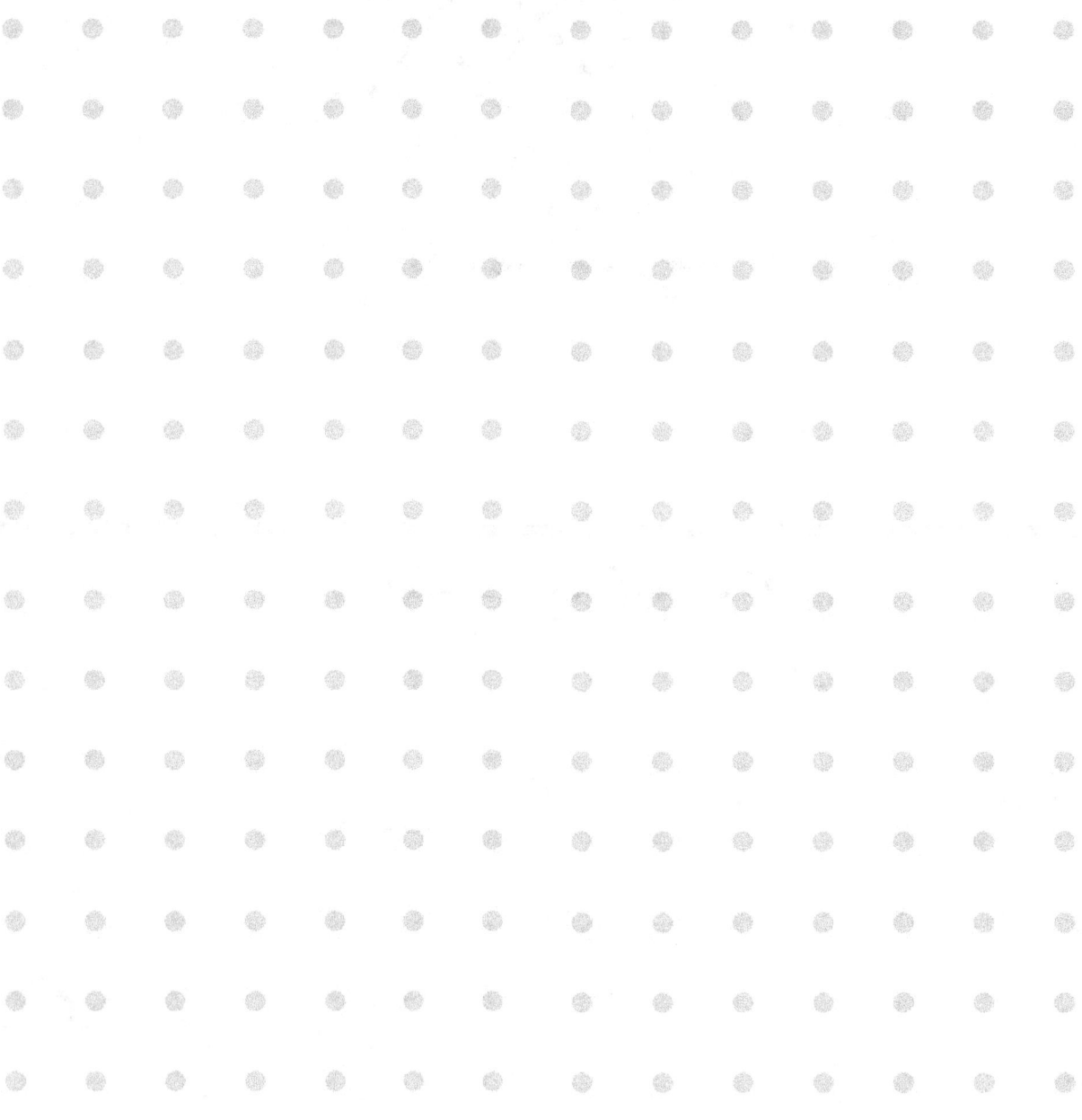

See this

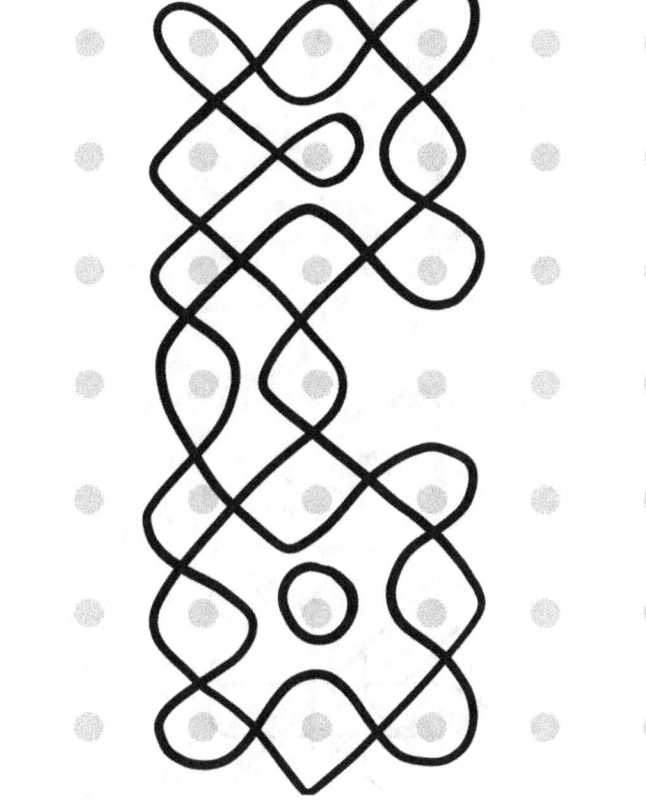

And draw here..

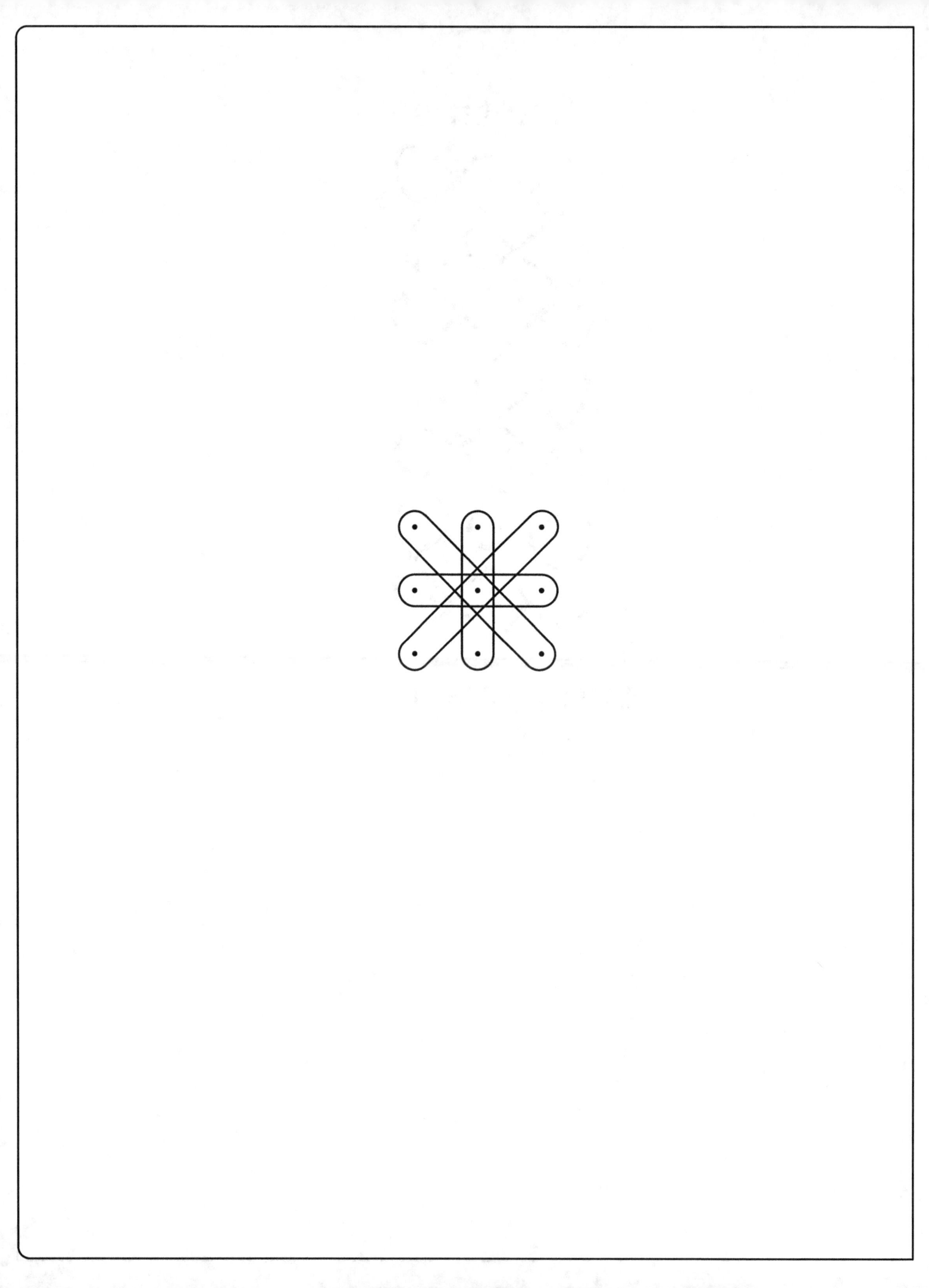

www.ingramcontent.com/pod-product-compliance
Lightning Source LLC
Chambersburg PA
CBHW081535220526
45467CB00010B/3196